No More Shadows: A Memoir

By Sherita Brandon

Street Affiliated Publishing

NO MORE SHADOWS: A MEMOIR BY SHERITA BRANDON

Editor: Shelby Lazenby
Join us on our social network pages:
Facebook
Author Sherita Brandon

Dedication

To My Parents: William *Billy* Washington and Mary *Cookie* Washington, who have passed on. May you continue to be my beacon of light and my strength.

To My Husband: Lorenzo X Brandon: For coming into my life and showering me with the greatest gift anyone could ever dream of: LOVE!

Acknowledgements

First and foremost, I would like to thank the God of my understanding, whom I choose to call Allah, for cleaning me up and taking me out my MESS to deliver a MESSage. All praises be unto Him!

To My Family: For just believing in me, trusting in me, and allowing me to be me. Aunt Jane and Linda, you are the best!

To Mr. Keith Williams: I've learned that God places people in your life when they need to be there. Thank you for watering the seed I planted many moons ago. Thanks for the *push* in getting me motivated to write this book. Also, thank you for the title and definition behind it.

To Author Larry Moon, Jr.: My sponsor and mentor. Thanks for believing in my and showing me the steps it takes to achieve this moment of success!

To My Editor: Shelby Lazenby: I thank you for your time and effort in pushing me to get this book out to the world. Your endless days and nights of going over my manuscript with a felt tip pen and a microscope (LOL).

To All My Supporters: Thank you for awesomeness! Your kindness will never be forgotten!

Thanks to all that have been with me on my journey. Thanks for showering me with never-ending love, especially Charlene, Bill Myrthil, and Momma Thurston. I love you bunches!

Shadow

A shadow cannot sustain an existence in the darkness, however with light it tracks. It follows and moves between the sources of illumination and the surface.

This phenomenon will reveal a silhouette of the object it shines upon.

My shadow has tracked me, followed me, stood beside me, and stood in front of but never moved until I motioned the movement.

This source of illumination reflecting off of me on the surface appeared to give my shadow life and/or an identity and energy of its own.

So, my shadow was who and what was seen and observed, but without my direction it couldn't move and was lifeless.

So how could one exist in a space where their representative is a is a reflection from an illumination of self.

Yet I choose to live in a place where the pain is less painful and numb.

Living in my shadow that I call the shade of life where I am identified by my movement not by who I truly am!

CHAPTER ONE

I always said I would write a book. I just never knew where to begin. I guess like where everything else starts I will begin from the beginning.

My birth name is Sherita Annette Washington. I was born on December 5th, 1965 at *Providence Hospital* in Washington, DC to the late William and Mary Washington. I don't recall a lot about my early childhood. I only recall what was told to me. I can say that I attended *Maryland Public Schools* while living in Palmer Park, Maryland under my Aunt Jane's roof. William Paca and Robert Frost were both predominately white schools, and I being a child of color, allowed this little Caucasian boy to cut off one of my ponytails because he said he liked me if he could cut my hair. I came home with one ponytail and my mother went ballistic! Needless to say, she was at the school first thing the next morning with me in tow looking like the black Pippi Longstocking. I can't tell you how my mother said she knew I would be a drunk because at the age of two. I would go around and drink everyone's unfinished liquor out their cups that was left on the table. I could also tell you that the pastor used to frequent our residence on Bryant Street Northwest, and I being drunk at two cursed him out.

Of course, all the adults thought that was the cutest thing. Now let's fast forward to now and I can begin to tell you my life story, starting at the age of thirteen when it all came tumbling down. I lived with my mother in *Southview Apartments* right off Southern Avenue in Oxon Hill, Maryland. I had a nice little summer job working right in the *Tiger Market Shopping Center* down the street from where we lived. To get to work was very accessible. All I had to do was cut through the wooded area by my building, and I would be at work. I can remember that day as if it were today. I got up early that morning, fed my cat, fixed breakfast, and watched a little television.

My mother was a person who had such a big heart and always looked out for others that sometimes she watched out for other's heart better than she watched out for her own. On this particular day, five guys whom I called my *brothers* came to visit. They ate breakfast, chilled out with me, and then went on their merry way. My mother always asked them to watch out for me, and they always vowed they would protect me. Not that day because I went to work at the McDonald's as I mentioned was my summer job, and then when I got off work I walked the trail which I took to work. That walk led me straight to my apartment building. In the midst of coming through the wooded area, I came across my five brothers who were loud, intoxicated, and singing old songs.

As I began to walk pass them, one of them grabbed me, and said, "Boy, Annette looks real good in her little work outfit."

Annette is my middle name. A name I used on the street because no one could seem to pronounce my government name correctly. Then the other four began to chime in and toss me back and forth. I really thought they were playing with me, but when I asked them to stop it did something to them. They threw me on the ground, and began to try and pull my pants down. I screamed, yelled, punched, and wiggled as I tried my damnedest to get away. However, I couldn't. Between their drunkenness and my fighting them to get them off me, they each raped me repeatedly. I could no longer cry. I was just numb.

When it was finally over, I made my way to my building. Once I got inside the apartment, I laid on the floor and cried endlessly. My mother finally came home from work and found me in the fetal position. When I told her what happened, she held and rocked me for a while. During her time of consoling me, she also told me that this should never be talked about again. I should never allow the rest of my family to know what happened to me. Secrets are all we had in our household. Go to the grave with that type of shit secrets.

My father was hardly around. The penitentiary was his home for many years and when he wasn't in prison or jail, he was at one of his other women's residence. He may have been married to my mother, but he played the field so much that my mother no longer cared if he came home. That's another story and I will get to that soon.

My mother washed me thoroughly and never reported the rape. She took me to see a psychiatrist. The sessions lasted for one full week, and then she felt that I was cured. Three weeks later, I find out I was pregnant and had contracted a venereal disease. I had to get a series of shots and an abortion. I was thirteen years old and I no longer knew what it was to feel like a teenager. My innocence was taken from me and it caused me to feel empty inside. I had no one to talk to since I was an only child, so I talked to myself a lot.

I always said, "If my father was here this would never have happened to me."

Then I would remember how my father was to my mother. He used to beat my mother so bad that when I got older, I vowed to kill him if he ever laid his hands on her again. He never did. So, I knew I wouldn't be going to a juvenile center until I was eighteen.

*****

We finally moved from that area and headed to *Randle Hill Apartments*, which were located on Sixth Street Southeast in the heart of the Congress Heights area. After a few months had passed, I started babysitting for my mother's bestfriend. She was gay, but I didn't know that she was. After all, she had two children. I thought that two men being together was gay. When I found out that women did it too, it kind of fascinated me. I wondered, *How do women be together because they can't do the things men do.* I was soon to find out that was a lie I told myself.

My mother's friend knew about me being raped and every time I was over to her house to babysit, she would always hug me and place a gentle kiss on my lips. I never thought too much about it until she invited me into her bedroom to see *something.* That something turned out to be a collection of dildos and other sex toys. She would fondle me, caress me, and hold me in her arms like she never wanted to let me go. Honestly, it felt good. It felt right. It felt too good!

She began to undress me slowly and methodically, like she was moving to a rhythm that she could only hear. Not wanting to disappoint her, I did as I was instructed to do by her and allowed her to have her way with me. She always said not to speak of this to anyone, especially my mother. We didn't want my mother to find out about the little game that we played. She would always give me a small amount of wine. She said it would help me get loose in order to be able to talk to her about all I was feeling and the things I could never talk to my mother about.

That went on for several months, and I actually felt a lot better. I was comfortable with talking to her and sharing my hurt, pain, and fears. I did all of that, not knowing I was in my most vulnerable stage and she would coldly take advantage of me. One evening, she called me over to her house to babysit. I went over but noticed the kids were gone. She said she just wanted a little time with me on her day off. I told her that was cool.

She was exploring places on me that I never knew existed. I didn't know what an orgasm was, I just knew it felt good. Since she was moaning, I moaned with her. My mother had left work early and always frequented her friend's house when she came home from work. This time when my mother visited, she had the shock of her life. When my mother walked through the front door all she could see was legs in the air and her friend's head between my legs. I was in shock, and I'm quite sure she was. My mother slammed the door. We jumped and I tried to cover

8

myself to the best of my ability.

My mother talked of kicking her friend's ass, and beating the shit out of me. All I could do was put my clothes on and run home. Once I got home, I decided that my mother was never going to try to run my life anymore. *That sounded real good coming from a thirteen year old doesn't it? Hell, at thirteen, what did I know about life?* I was just beginning to live my life. I began to pack a suitcase so I could go live with my mother's friend.

Once I got back to her friend's apartment, I saw that things became heated up. They had gotten into a physical altercation, which left her friend defenseless.

My mother noticed that I had a suitcase in hand, and asked, "Where do you think you're going?"

I said, "Here to be with your friend."

I yelled out that I loved her and would never part from her, and then it was like the scene from *The Color Purple* where Celie was all packed and ready to go with Shug Avery. My mother was furious. Her friend began to tell me that she was going back to Ohio and what she did to me was wrong. She told me about how she was selfish when it concerned her own feelings, and that she never realized that she was damaging me more.

I flew out the house in a rage and went down to the playground where people were smoking and drinking. I blended in well and had my first use of alcohol and marijuana. Back then it was called reefer, and I just knew that was the start of something good. I smoked damn near every day. I was choking from the smoke and catching the munchies. I would sneak in the house, take money from my mother's purse or her little bank, and then find people who could purchase the reefer and alcohol to get me started.

*****

Summertime, 1978, was wonderful but now it was time to get back into the books. I began school at Hart Junior High School. I left the problems of the summer behind me and looked forward to excelling in sports. I ran track and field, and I was very good at it. In fact, the coach at that time said he could envision me in the Olympics. *Me in the Olympics as a track and field star?* Yes, I felt I could live out that dream. It was accessible and obtainable. I could be the next Flo Jo.

I got into so many fights that I got kicked out of school. I was defending people who I called my friends, but none of them were ever there to defend me. My mother had me enrolled into Assumption Catholic School. *I was like really, a freaking Catholic school? How was that supposed to work for me?* I always thought Catholics were Roman Caucasians and hypocritical people. *What did I know?* I was a Baptist. I had just heard so many things about Catholics that I shunned them. I didn't want to go to a Catholic school, wearing a uniform, looking like everyone else, and not being able to be who I really was. I was really an out of control teenager.

That's when I knew my career as a track and field star was over. Catholic schools didn't have track and field, at least not this one anyway. They offered tap dancing, ballet, science club, and a spelling bee. I signed up for the spelling bee because I was a damn good speller and loved English. I knew I could do that. I actually came in third place in the Knights of Columbus Spelling Bee Contest. I can even remember beating the smartest boy in our class. That was a victory for me.

Yeah, I could do the Catholic school thing. I met some of the coolest people there. They had their after school sports too. They had drinking and smoking. Yeah, that was my kind of crew. I knew that I would fit in perfectly. I would go to school twisted every day, not knowing when it began or ended. All I knew was that I couldn't wait to get home and relax with a joint and a drink. My mother worked two jobs, so it was easy for me to do the things that I wanted to do.

I wasn't into boys, so I always seemed to hang out with the girls. I tried to get close to them to see if by chance, they swung the way that I did. I found one girl in the bunch that would be with me as long as I provided her with drugs to get high and drinks. That was no problem. The money I had banked from working began to come in handy. Finding a dealer was no problem as long as you had the money, and he provided me with the best weed ever.

My grades began to spiral downhill, but I still managed to graduate from junior high school and attend The Academy of Notre Dame, which was located on North Capitol and K Street Northwest. It was connected to the all boy school, Gonzaga. I really wasn't feeling that freshmen year at a new school. I wanted to go to public school and hang out with some cool people. There were only two girls from Assumption that were enrolled at Notre Dame with me. We didn't hang out, but nonetheless we were alright with each other.

Entering into this new dimension took me for a loop. We use to have to meet in a cafeteria across the street where the seniors would pick a little sister, a freshman, and guide them through the ropes of the school. Meeting with them, talking to them, or hanging out with them was not for me. I didn't need any senior cramping my style.

Unfortunately, I was hooked up with this Caucasian girl. She wasn't popular or anything. She was just a regular plain Jane. She showed me around the school, introduced me to her friends, and told me the activities I should sign up for in my first year of high school. I signed up for the drill team and track and field. I really wasn't feeling any of that stuff. I was so use to people telling me what to do and how to do things. It never occurred to me to think for myself. I just wanted to be a likable person. I desperately wanted to make friends.

I wasn't the cutest person, but I also wasn't I the ugliest. I have a birthmark on the right side of my face. When you first look at it, you would think I have a black eye. I hate that birthmark. My mother said I received it from her being scalded with a bowl of greens that she was eating when her brother jumped out and scared her. The bowl flew up to her face and burned the right side. Whenever people came in contact with me that would be the first thing that they notice then they started to ask question. It was always, *Who blacked your eye or who beat you up?* I was so damn tired of telling the story of my birthmark.

As the school year kicked off, having to be involved with extracurricular activities and doing a lot of homework, my grades miraculously picked up. I was able to excel, momentarily. One day I decided to hang out with a bunch of yuppie girls, and they introduced me to acid. Boy was that a kicker! I never knew a high could be so great! The euphoria was surreal. I placed that strip on my tongue and let it dissolve then just sat back and waited. As I waited, I began to see my friend's curtains melting. I thought, *Wow, holy shit!* I got up from the couch and walked towards the curtains and began to pick up the stripes that were hitting the floor so fast that I could hardly keep up.

Low and behold, my friend came out the room, and asked, "What are you doing?"

I told her, "I'm picking your curtains up and trying to put them back together."

What a load of laughs I received that night. By the time I got home, I was tee totally wasted. I don't remember anything after that. I woke up and it was time to get showered and ready for school. I noticed that my mother wasn't in, so I didn't have to explain to her why I was throwing up all over the place. After cleaning up my mess, I prepared for another day of school and wondered what that day would bring.

Soon as I walked in the cafeteria, I was the most talked about person there. I felt so humiliated. I just wanted to run and hide. I left the cafeteria in tears. I can remember some young lady standing outside by the bus stop talking about how the girls of Notre Dame are whores to the Gonzaga boys. I thought, *Really?* Little did she know I was a Notre Dame girl. I said something smart to her, and then I walked off.

By the time I crossed the street, I saw one of the sisters standing in the front of the building. I wanted to duck her but she noticed me, and I had no choice but to go in that dreary building. I was sent to the office to see the Mother Supreme. I guess that's what you call her. She had some words for me, and I in turn had some words for her. She paddled me, and I told her that was the biggest mistake she could have ever made. I left the building, caught the bus home, and called my mother at work to tell her what had happened. I failed to mention that I had cursed the sister out for raising her voice at me and definitely for paddling me. My mother wasn't hearing any of it.

First thing in the morning, we were in route to see the Mother Supreme and her flunkies. My mother didn't waste any time in saying what needed to be said. All I can really remember is being escorted from the school by the police and a voice saying that I was expelled indefinitely. I figured oh well because I'd had enough of the Catholics and their rules and regulations. I just was waiting to hear the magic words from my mother's lips. Those words didn't come when I wanted them to, in fact, they came after she had a meeting with the tuition people and was refunded her money for the remaining of the school year.

When my mother came home she still had an attitude because she had to take off work, but was relieved it was taken care of. Good riddance to Notre Dame! After dinner that evening, my mother said we were getting up the next morning and going to get me enrolled at Ballou. I almost couldn't contain my excitement. I was happy to be going back to public school. I already knew I was going to be involved in a lot of activities. I was just glad I would be given a little more freedom.

I got through the rest of the school year without any problems. Summertime was here and it was time to make it do what it do! Most of my friends went to Ballou, so it wasn't hard to get adjusted and find my way around. It was the school year of 1980, and I was going in full swing. It was my sophomore year and things were going well until I was introduced to hash. I thought to myself, *What in the world is that? How do you smoke it if you're not rolling it up like reefer?*

My house seemed like the *get high* place for everyone. My mother was always working, so I was on my own a lot. One particular day, I remember sitting on my couch with about five of us sitting in front of a drinking glass. One of my friends took a safety pin, put the block of Hash on it, burned it and placed the glass over it. All you could see was a lot of smoke. Each of us took turns lifting the glass and sucking up the smoke. It seemed alright in the beginning, but I figured I would stick to the reefer. I got up and fixed us some food. Once we finished eating, we went back to school in time to make fifth period.

The day seemed to be dragging on, but somehow I made it through. I had joined the marching band. I played the snare drum and also got on the swim team. I ran track for a while, but my career ended with a torn ligament in my right knee. I believe I performed one time with the marching band before I was kicked off because of being high and disorderly conduct. I cursed everyone out. I just didn't care anymore. I figured screw the marching band, I could become a pep squad girl or a cheerleader.

I was on the pep squad for about a month, and then I decided that I would devote myself to swimming. I placed first place in the breaststroke and freestyle. I enjoyed swimming. It kind of took me away from being where I was at the time. I felt free but lonely. I use to sit on the bleachers and think of my mother's old friend. I missed her really bad. I even tried to find out where she was living. I thought that maybe I could go and visit her.

Just as I was gathering my belongings and about to get up and leave the bleachers, a strong voice behind me asked, "Would you like some company?"

I turned and looked at him. It seemed like I sat there forever and no words seemed to escape my lips. He introduced himself as Brian. He was short, brown-skinned, and he had wavy hair. *What did this cutie want from me?* He sat down, pulled out a joint, fired it up, and then he began to speak so eloquently. I asked him did he attend Ballou and he answered was no. Brain told me that he just had a lot of friends up that way and he always came out to the bleachers to *clear his head.*

I thought to myself, *Cool, I have another get high partner*. That was just what I needed. We talked for a long time. He told me he was from Barry Farms. Right then, I put my mental brakes on. Barry Farms was one of the toughest neighborhoods in Southeast DC. You couldn't even get into Barry Farms unless you knew someone, and they had to meet you at the top of the hill to escort you.

After the bell rung, letting me know school was being dismissed, I thanked him for the smoke and was on my way. He grabbed me by the arm and asked me for my phone number. I asked for his phone number and said I would call him. He walked me to the gate, and then lingered behind. I guess he was waiting on his friends to come out. As I walked the couple of blocks home, I could do nothing but think of my mother's friend and how this boy was trying to get to know me.

I really didn't know how to tell him that I was not interested in guys. I was gay and my lover lived in Ohio. She was so many miles away that he was complicating things right now, but damn he was fine as all outdoors! I thought that maybe it would not have hurt just to talk to him on the phone.

It took me two days to call him. We talked like we had known each other forever. It seemed like I could talk to him about anything, except being gay. I just couldn't let anyone know that about me, and I mean no one.

Late that evening after dinner, I sat on the bed with my princess telephone and dialed his number. He was quick to answer as if he'd been waiting by the phone for my call. We talked for a few minutes and we both promised that we would see each other the next day. I can remember waiting for the sun to come up, so that I could see what the next day would bring.

After getting up early, showering, and fixing breakfast, I lingered back a moment. I was waiting for my mother to leave for work. I had no plans of going to school. I just wanted to chill at home with a few friends, get high, eat, and talk shit. I called Brian and gave him my address so that he could come over and hangout. It beat the bleachers any day of the week.

When he arrived, after my other friends, I felt a little uneasy. I kind of liked him, but I didn't like him like that if that makes any sense. He was a clingy type of guy. He always had to lean on me or whisper shit in my ear. It was kind of an invasion of personal space. He leaned over and kissed me soft, but with passion. I went along with it. As time moved on, so did my friends.

Bidding me a good evening and our promise of meeting up with each other the next day, Brian stayed longer and when he finally said his goodbyes it was time for me to fix dinner. My mother was coming home shortly and I wanted to ensure her a nice hot meal after a long day of work. I called a classmate of mines to get the homework assignment, so I can be on point at school the next day. There had been many days that I would miss from school, but I could always show up with my homework assignments and take the tests and pass. I kind of prided myself on that. My report card spoke for itself. I would always find a way to change my absences, so that my mother wouldn't be alarmed and find out that I spent most my days away from school.

CHAPTER TWO

Sophomore year was a blast! I came and went as I pleased and before I knew it, it was time for summer break. I couldn't wait to hit the pools, go skating, and to the go-go's. I had always skated in Alexandria, Virginia. I even joined the skate team called *Mr. B's Delights*. I loved to skate. The competition was the highlight of my weekends. I would twist, turn, skate backwards, forwards, and do spins. I was in a zone when I got on the rink.

Afterwards, we would head up Georgetown and watch the Spanish guys breakdance and pop dance, or head over to Paragon Two. It was so cool. Most Saturdays if we weren't skating, we would head up to New York Avenue, across from the Greyhound Bus Station, to *The Room* to hear DJ Kool spin the records and get our drink on. My favorite drink was a Singapore sling or a long island ice tea. Those would definitely set me right.

As I was making my way to the dance floor, who did I bump into? It was Brian in the flesh. He was flossing. Brian had on his Kangol outfit. He was too smooth to move. He would just sway from side-to-side. He asked if I needed a ride home and I declined, letting him know I was with friends. He said he would like to spend some quality time with me. I knew what that meant. He wanted to get into my pants, but I wasn't ready for that. All my friends were actively involved in sex, but I wasn't after being raped. I had wiped sex clear from my vocabulary until a week later then I finally gave in. He was very gentle with me. He did the foreplay stuff and all of that. I thought it would be a wham, bam, thank you ma'am type of night, but it wasn't. He even took me home, walked me to my building, and gave me a kiss. He said he wanted me to meet his mother. I was asking myself, *Why?* This wasn't going to be a long-term relationship, but in fact it lasted longer than I expected.

Entering my junior year, there had been some major changes in Brian's attitude. I saw that he was jealous of anyone I came in contact with. He wanted me to lose my friends and only be around him. I had to constantly remind him that I was a student, and he was just a passerby. These people he wanted me to rid myself of were truly my friends. It came days that he would gain entrance into the school. He would roam the halls until he found one of my friends in order to find out what class I was in or he would just ask random people if they had seen me. Everyone knew he was my boyfriend, so they felt it was okay for him to know where I was. I can recall coming out of my English class and talking to one of the guys about the assignment, which was given to us and out of nowhere here, Brian came.

BAM!

There was a smack to my face, and then I was on the ground. My books were knocked everywhere and people in the hall just looked at us. All I can remember was Brian constantly accusing me of cheating. I couldn't believe that mess.

Really? Cheating? What or who gave him that idea? It didn't matter whether I was with a male or female because I was always accused. As I tried to gather my books and other belongings up from the floor, he grabbed me by my ponytail and dragged me down the hall. Security was no match for him. They had to call the 7th District to get him off and away from me. I even had staff members drive me home. I got a stay away order on him, but he didn't care about that. He continued to bother and harass me.

He came to my building that evening. My mother still wasn't home from work. He yelled and screamed my name. He banged on our patio window, being that we were on the first floor. When I didn't answer, he took a brick and broke our patio window. I called the police and ran to the neighbor's house and waited until they arrived. The police asked if I wanted to press charges, and he kept yelling that I would be sorry if I did. I just wanted that to be over. *How was I going to tell my mother that this boy smashed her window in with a brick because he was jealous?* Brian kept yelling that he was sorry, and he said he wouldn't do it again. He begged me to come to the police station and tell them that it was all a big misunderstanding.

First things first, I had to call the rental office and tell them that the glass was busted and needed to be replaced. Maintenance came and put up a wooden board until the next day when they would be able to replace it, and that was money out of my pocket. My mother was coming down the walkway as all that mess was unfolding, and I didn't like the look I saw in her eyes. She was fussing and cursing, and she even went over to the police car and told Brian she should kill him. He begged my mother for forgiveness then she just turned and walked away.

I slept in the front room that night. I was just waiting for the sun to come up. I already knew school wasn't an option for me. There was too much shit that needed to be done. The phone was ringing, and actually woke me from my slumber. It was a call from Brian.

"Can you not show up to court?" he asked of me.

If I didn't show up they would drop the charges, and he could come home. I figured that since he apologized and said he would never do it again things would get better. I didn't go to the court hearing. I really wasn't thinking about court.

That just made me think of the relationship my parents had. I would watch my father beat my mother until she was black and blue. She would have bruises all up and down her arms and back. Her legs showed a lot of discoloration from the falls she had taken. I can also remember how she would say that he didn't mean it. He would say that he was having a bad day.

She told me that my father really did love her. He was just falling on some hard times. She said I shouldn't hold any of this against him, but I hated my father. I wanted him to be dead. The only thing that saved my father from death was jail and prison.

My father would take my mother's money and leave, knowing it was rent time. He never bothered to worry about whether we would have a roof over our head or food in our mouths. As long as he got what he wanted, Billy was okay. Whenever he was discharged from jail or prison, he would never make it home to us. He would run for cover to his sister's house, who was my aunt, his baby sister, and his sole enabler until his untimely death.

*****

Being with Brian had its perks. I got high for free and was able to experiment with different drugs. He introduced me to PCP, which was a drug that has you stripping out your clothes. It was originally called butt naked because that's how it leaves you feeling after you smoke it. It leave you in a zombie state. It was marijuana laced with embalming fluid, so people who smoked it were out of their minds.

My first hit of it made me forget where I was. I mean, I could literally be sitting on the back porch smoking and once I was done. I would take a look around and it seemed like I was in another place and time. I would think I was walking straight, but it had me lifting my feet so high off the ground that it was as if the sidewalk had jumped up in my face. I would be so high that I would get into fights and end up in jail, not knowing what the hell went on.

Brian had left a few packages with me one day. I took them to school. I got high on the bleachers and into a fight that involved a teacher, and then I was suspended. Here it was my junior year, and I was acting like a complete ass. It really didn't bother me much. I really didn't care if I finished high school or not. My mother use to always tell me I wasn't shit, and that I would never amount to anything. She said that I would grow up to be just like my daddy and locked away in prisons.

My mother always said my daddy wanted a boy. My mother had always said if her first child was a girl that it was for her. Needless to say, she upheld that to her grave. So, there I was, getting higher and higher to escape the pain I was feeling. Knowing my mom had to go up to the school to resolve the issue at hand was something I dreaded. The best thing that came from that was that I wasn't arrested on for that incident, but it was soon to come. My mom talked with the principal and the teacher involved and came to the decision that I needed professional help. She said that I needed to get into anger management and take drug classes. I wasn't angry and I damn sure didn't have a drug problem. I could stop at any time.

Upon completion of the drug classes and anger management, I was able to go back to school. I was placed on a probationary period, which consisted of me not missing any classes, me turning in all homework assignments, and me having at least seventy-five percent participation in all my classes. I managed to do that for about three weeks before I started the black national anthem and said fuck it then left.

With a few more weeks before report cards were due to come out, I gave up on school. My mother said if I didn't go to school, I need to find myself another place to live. I asked myself, *Where can I go? What mother does that to her only child?* I couldn't let that happen. I went to school, faced the disciplinary board, and to my astonishment I had passed all my classes. I went home, got high, and celebrated. I listened to, *Party Time*, by Kurtis Blow and danced my ass off.

My mother came home with her friend, Jose, and when I showed her my final report card she was most pleased. She saw that I was high, but said nothing. I called a couple of my friends over and we sat in my room and got twisted. My mother called for me to ask me if I knew where to get a bag of weed from. I said yes. I was so high that I took a bag from my purse and handed it to her with my palm extended for the cash. She asked if I was selling weed, and I said not exactly. I just told her that I happened to have an extra bag on me. She gave me the ten dollars and went on to her room.

Jose was in the kitchen acting like he was a scientist. He was mixing chemicals up to make his angel dust and loveboat, and I was on standby to receive his gifts. Jose always seemed to leave containers of angel dust and loveboat in the freezer and without a doubt. I'm sure he knew I was dabbing in it. In the beginning all I would take out is enough to roll up a joint. Then I began to take the whole sack. My friends and I left out, promising my mother I would be in early. We walked to the liquor store, got a couple of beers, and then we went and sat on the benches at the *Congress Heights Park and Recreation Center*. We got high and drank as we watched the guys play basketball and some play tennis.

As we were getting ready to leave, Brian showed up and wanted to argue. Mind you that I'm so high that I barely even knew what he was talking about until he smacked me clean across the park table. I got up with my nose bleeding and stunned. My friends were trying to block him from hitting me then he pulled out his gun. They all backed away. I told them to go ahead of me, and that I would be okay. One of my friends wanted to stay with me. Brian told her if she didn't leave he would blow her head off then mine. I begged her to go. Reluctantly, she left. He told her if the police showed up, she would regret the day she was born.

He asked where have I been, and why haven't I called. I explained to him that I had to build my grades up and didn't need any distractions. That didn't come out well. He smacked me again.

"So, now I'm a distraction!" he yelled!

I just kept quiet. He smacked me in the head with the butt of his gun and told me to get to walk to the bus stop. I told him I wanted to go home, and he said I was going with him. Brain said that he would tell me when I could leave. He questioned me about my friends, all of whom were girls. If we were screwing each other it didn't matter because he had heard that I had been with a woman before.

I explained to him that when I was with a woman, I didn't have to worry about being beaten. *Why didn't I just keep my big mouth shut?* Brain beat and stomped me by the bus stop then left me there. Someone called the ambulance and called my mother to inform her I was beaten bad. Brian had left the scene. My mother and Jose came to the hospital, and the police questioned my mother. There was nothing they could do unless I spoke up, and I refused. I knew that if I ever spoke about this incident that I would wind up dead.

I remained in the hospital for a week with bruised ribs and a concussion. I also had five stitches to my right eye. I was sore as shit. My mother came each day after work to check on me. My friends also came after school. Everyone kept telling me to leave Brain, but I knew the consequences. I said I would leave him just for them all to switch subjects.

I came home on a Friday. I remember that because it was my friend's birthday and she was having a party on Saturday. Jose had left me some money to go get a few outfits and shoes, and I even had enough money to get my friend an outfit for her birthday. We headed downtown to go shopping. When we got to the Martin Luther King Avenue we saw Brian and what seemed to be like half of the 7th District of police officers. They were locking him up. It was as if he could smell me. He looked up then our eyes locked, and I read his lips to come bail him out. My friend nudged me to come on but I couldn't seem to get my feet to go. I nodded to Brain, turned from my friend and told her I was going to bail him out.

Everyone thought I was crazy. I had to remind one of my friends that she had always went to bat for her boyfriend no matter how many times we tried to get her to leave him. I even had it in with my mother for allowing my dad to beat her so much. She never left. The only thing that saved my mother was my father going to do time somewhere.

As I headed to 7th District with my outfit money in my pocket, all I could think was what could I do to keep Brian happy and not make him feel he had to be jealous. I was never one to flirt around or flaunt myself, even though I'd always been told that if you have it you should flaunt it. That was an old folk saying and I just never really understood it until later in life.

I walked into the police station, and to my surprise Brian was being released. It was a case of mistaken identity. This boy must have had a horseshoe up his ass or he knew someone in high places. I told him I was going to go to the party and he said he wanted to go. I couldn't tell him my friend didn't want him there. That would be another argument/fight, and I didn't have the strength for any of it. Instead, I suggested we just go to the movies and go back to his place and chill. Brain agreed.

The night was going great. His mother was there when we arrived. She was one of the sweetest ladies I have ever met. Like any mother she thought her child could do no wrong. Whenever I talked to her about Brian, she would tell me that he would get better. She thought he just needed to take his meds. He hadn't been the same since he witnessed his father getting gunned down. It was a drug deal gone bad, and Brian was about eight years old when it took place. His mother told me how she tried to get him to take his meds and see the psychiatrist, but it never worked out.

When Brian entered the living room where we were it got eerily quiet. He knew something was amidst. I told him I was sorry to hear about his dad and when I hugged him, he seemed to tense up to my touch. I knew Brain was fighting back the tears, and he just grabbed my hand and we went to his room. We played music and just laid there listening to each other breath until we both fell asleep.

I got up pretty early and had to rush home because I had to go to church. If I didn't go to church, I would never hear the end of it. I attended *Rehoboth Baptist Church* and sang in the young adult choir. Whenever we sand was the only time I really liked going to church service. That was when I was most happy. I believed in God, but I just never really exercised my faith. I was looking for a God that would be like the one they talked about in the Bible. The one who turned water into wine, healed the lepers, healed those who were blind to allowed them to see, and raised the dead. *Where was this Almighty God when I needed Him?* I needed Him to take away the pain I was feeling. I needed Him to heal my broken heart, and fix my boyfriend. I needed Him to raise Brain's dad from the dead, so that he can feel whole again.

Every Sunday, I went to that alter and prayed but still nothing happened. That's when I figured God had passed me by. I went home from service, feeling emptier than I'd ever felt before. I just laid on my bed and cried. I cried so much that I got sick to my stomach. My head was pounding and I needed to find some relief. I went into the bathroom to get some Ibuprofen from the medicine cabinet, and figured I needed to eat something as well. I looked in the freezer and saw those tupperware bowls. I knew what was in there, I just needed one sack to make everything all right.

I looked in the refrigerator to get some water, but figured a beer would do me justice. I changed into some shorts, a T-shirt, my sandals, and then went up to the recreation center to get my buzz on. I thought to myself, *Damn, I don't have any cigarettes or lighter.* I walked to the corner store and got what I needed then just chilled. I sat out there until it was turning dark.

Knowing that I had school the next day, I went on home high as hell but my headache gone.

I felt like shit when I woke up the next morning. I showered and got myself ready to leave for school when a knock came at my door. It was all my get high buddies with something new for me to try. I hurried and got dressed, informing them I had to leave in about forty-five minutes. That would give me enough time to make it to school for homeroom attendance. I came into the living room and all I saw was a glass mirror with white powder all over it in lines. I saw my friends taking turns bending over with a dollar bill rolled up and sniffing up the powder.

I asked, "What the fuck is that?"

One of them answered, "You're really a square. It's powdered cocaine.

"What? What does it do? Why do you sniff it?" I questioned, and then my turn came.

I took one sniff and the heaven's opened up. I'm sure my crossed and by the time I realized what time it was it was lunchtime. I couldn't believe that we had been snorting coke half of the day. I felt real good. This was a feeling I never wanted go or leave. My friend sold me a twenty-dollar bag and they all left. I was left in my apartment with a high I never wanted to lose. I took the clear bag to my room, left it on the dresser, and just laid back to relax. Turned on the TV and never knew what I was watching. In fact, the TV was watching me. I felt my high coming down and wanted to be lifted up again, so I snorted the bag I had purchased, and then I began to clean the house.

I was doing shit I had never thought of doing and when my mother came home, she seemed to always be able to detect when I was misbehaving. She asked me what was I so skied up on, and I said nothing. She looked me in my face and wiped my nose with her finger.

My mother asked, "Where did you get cocaine from?"

I asked, "What cocaine? You crazy, I don't have any cocaine."

She began her search and there in my room on the dresser, she found my little clear bag with a little substance in it. She didn't say anything else. My mother took the bag then went into her room and closed the door. I didn't know what to think, say, or do. I did what I thought was best and I lift. I stayed over my friend house that lived in the next building from me. I got up early enough in the morning to go home, shower, and get to school. Luckily, my mother had left and I was still worried about what was to come of the lie I had told her.

I went to school, dragging and feeling like crap. I saw a couple of my friends that I hung out with. They all asked if I was coming to swimming practice and I said no. I had other obligations. I planned to get my hair braided after school, and then to get to bed early. I needed to get back on track. I just needed a pick me up. I had my friend meet me and I gave her fifty dollars for some coke.

This time I knew I had to find a place to hide it so that my mother wouldn't find it. I went to get my hair done and when I got home my mother was on the phone. She was talking loud, and I kept asking what was wrong. When my mother hung up, she looked at me and said Jose had been shot. My mother said that she had to get to the hospital to see him. I said okay, and then she left. I laid on the couch listening to some music, wondering who would shoot Jose and why.

I took the bag of coke from my pocket and went into the kitchen to get a straw and some scissors. I cut the straw in an angle, poured some of the coke onto the small compact mirror, and then snorted my heart out. The euphoria was awesome. I was in another world. I fixed something to eat and went into my room, waiting to hear from my mom and Jose.

My mom came home a few hours later with some devastating news. Jose is dead. *What? What did she say?* I asked myself again and again. She repeated herself and I just crumbled over. Jose was like the father I wished I had. Jose treated my mother good. He treated me and my friends good. Jose provided for us. He was always a phone call away. I cried out to God, asking myself and Him, *Why? Why would you always take all the good people away from me?* I just couldn't understand that.

*****

I didn't go to school the next day. I laid in my room. I snorted my coke, smoked boat, and drank alcohol. My mother didn't go to work. She went to Jose's mother's house to see how she was doing and spent some time with her and his son. All I could think about is how that little boy was going to grow up, not knowing much about his father. His mother wasn't in his life. The only one close to Jose as a mother figure was my mom and his grandmother.

Brian called me, and I told him what happened. He came right over. He held me and rocked me. It seemed like he would never let me go. These were the times when I really enjoyed being with him. I finally went home after a couple of days, knowing I needed to get to school.

CHAPTER THREE

The next year would be my senior year and I had a lot to do to get there. I found myself walking towards the school, but just never making it inside. I went to my favorite spot, which was the bleachers on the field where I smoked and smoked and smoked. I smoked to fill the void of emptiness inside.

Jose was gone and I was left with an empty feeling. He was the best thing that came into my mother's life. As I was sitting there, I heard a voice behind me. I didn't know if I was tripping or if it were an actual voice. Yes, it was the principal, Dr. Dennis Johnson, better known as Dr. J.

Dr. Johnson would get on the P.A. system every day to encourage the students to do better, and end by saying that it was another day, another A, and to go all the way with Dr. J! This man would follow students to the store, making sure no one bought alcohol. If they did, he would pour it out, saying it clouds your judgement. I wish I had listened back then.

When Dr. Johnson approached me, he said that I was high. He told me I still had time to get my stuff together if I wanted to be promoted to be a senior. Of course I did. Dr. Johnson encouraged me to go home, get some rest, and then he would see me in his office first thing the next day. I obliged. I went home, showered, ate, and went to sleep. I rested real good. I woke up feeling refreshed. My mother wasn't there, and I wasn't going to call her. I really didn't need to be depressed when I went to school.

I met with Dr. Johnson and my credits were good. I just needed to pass the final exams in Trigonometry, English III, and American Literature then I would be a senior. I studied extra hard when I really didn't need to, but I just wanted to throw myself into something to keep me occupied. After a few weeks had passed, test time was beginning. I went into those classes with a lot of zeal, knowing I would let nothing stand in my way.

I finished my last exam, gathered my belongings, and left the building. Brian was outside to meet me. He walked me home and stayed with me for a while. I finally called my mother, who told me she was okay and on her way home. She said that Grandma Emma was okay and little Cordie was doing well. I was happy to hear that. When my mother came home she was with some big dude named Ray. She said something about going to a baseball game that night. I was trying to figure out who in the hell plays baseball at nine PM, and where that game was at. It wasn't until later that I found out that *baseball game* was freebasing and she would be gone all night, getting home just in time to wash and get herself ready for work.

I went on to school and went directly to homeroom. An announcement came across the P.A. system, asking all the juniors to report to the auditorium for an update on the final exams. My heart sank. All I could think of was why didn't I smoke a joint or sniff some coke before coming to hear that shit. I was nervous as hell and really didn't want to go to an assembly early in the freaking morning.

As I walked in along with some of my friends, the auditorium was surprisingly empty. *Did the juniors come to school today? Was this a joke just to see who would show up or who wouldn't?* I sat in the back. My friends moseyed up towards the front. I could be humiliated from the back. Maybe a hundred, if that many people, showed up. They announced individually the students in their class and what they made on the exam. I sunk down in my seat. Since my last name was Washington, I already knew I would be last.

The names rolled by quickly and it was then and there that I realized, I would be a senior in nineteen eighty-one and graduate in nineteen eighty-two! I passed with flying colors. My G.P.A. was three point eight and I was on my way. I left the auditorium elated and went home to celebrate. I wanted to find out about this baseball game, freebasing stuff. My friends were already doing it. I was just so caught up into other things, not to be involved until I was anxious

25

to see what I've been missing.

I went over a friend's house. They showed me a glass bowl, some chore boy, a lighter, and a white rock, which they explained was cocaine cooked up to a solid ball. I was at a loss for words. I was wondering how this was supposed to work out. I watched and waited. When it finally came to me, I was nervous but once I hit that rock and saw the smoke hit the bottom and fill that glass bowl up, all I had to do was to inhale that smoke, and all my problems seemed to wash away. I heard bells ringing, my ears got clogged up, and I felt like I was on a cloud. Thar was the high I'd been looking for.

I dished out money and bought all the stuff I needed to fulfill my need for that new high. We smoked and smoked and spent and spent until all I knew was that I needed more. I went home, showered, changed clothes, and went to the bank. I withdrew two hundred dollars and started all over again. My friend told me about the money she was making by selling the drug, and I said I would think about it. I knew I wanted to get my hands on that. To be able to sell the drugs and get high and not use my money, per se, was a path I was willing to go down. *I was so use to trying everything, why not that?*

Before I knew it, summer was over and it was time to head back to school. I already knew I wasn't going to be there long. I filled out papers to go to Job Corps. I was still at Ballou for a few months, and my boyfriend continued to come there and terrorize me. I told him I was leaving and going to Keystone, Pennsylvania to Job Corps and our relationship was over. He beat me senseless, and told me I wasn't going anywhere. I said that I would remain in DC where he could keep his eyes on me. I never wanted to be far away from home, in fear I would miss out on the action.

I attended *Potomac Job Corps Center* and took up the trade of cement masonry. I could get my G.E.D. there, while learning a trade. I took Job Corps by storm. I was enrolled in the G.E.D. program, but just never found the need to attend. I felt that finishing up cement masonry was a better option for me towards getting employed than finishing my education at that time. I sold drugs there and made a lot of money while still being able to keep up my habit.

I didn't live far from the center, so it was easy for me to meet my connection and make the tradeoff. I became the *face of the place* and no one could sell anything there without my knowledge. I banked enough money to get my own stuff and still managed to work construction and keep up with my business. It began to boom at the center and I had the head lady looking to other residents for information. No one seemed to be giving her any information about me, but I laid low.

I had to start trusting other people to handle the business, and I just collected the money. It started flourishing fast, and I knew I was going to be a major seller in the cocaine industry. I began going with friends to their houses in Baltimore, Philadelphia, and New York over the weekends. I was learning more about the coke business. I learned how to receive the best deals and the good quality product.

I came home one weekend to find my mother and her friends getting high. I gave them a sample of my product, and they started buying from me. That would be the first time me and my mother got high together. I always said that once you cross the line there's no turning back. My mother was no longer a parent in my eyesight. She became a get high partner. She would buy from me like anyone else and get treated the same way others were treated. If she got a credit, she was to pay me like anyone else. After all, this was a business.

One night we were getting high, and she actually took a packet from me. I questioned her about it and she lied. I drew my hand back and was ready to strike her, and that's when I knew it was time for me to leave my mother's place. I went in my room and packed a suitcase then I left. I heard her crying out my name, but I just couldn't look at her anymore. The drugs had finally come between us and our household. I stayed with a friend that night, promising to leave in the morning to find a room. I found a room in the tourist home on Parkland Place Southeast. The lady that worked there got high, so as long as I supplied her with drugs she was okay. I even bought her food and drinks, and I was able to stay there as long as I wanted.

I knew I had to return to Job Corps to face what lied ahead in my future. I got there and was detained in the office. It was bought to my attention that someone had set fire to my closet while I was away. I already knew one of my roommates didn't like me, and I figured it was her. All I needed was to see her, and I already knew what I was going to do her. They sent me back home until they got things in order and said I could return in two weeks. They told me that they would write a report, process it, and send me to *Sears* where they had an account to get the things replaced. I informed them that my clothing didn't come from Sears, and that I would give them an itemized list of my belongings so they could cut me a check and I could buy my items myself.

Once everything was processed, I was discharged from Job Corps and had to return to the tourist home. I was making money steadily and banking it until one day when the police ran in and busted the tourist home. That was my first time being locked up, and the only person I could call was Brian. I told him that the charges were possession, possession with intent to distribute, and distribution. There wasn't much found, so I was able to get out personal recognizance. Brian met me at the courthouse and demanded to know where I got the coke from. I wasn't feeling all that from him. It was mine and mine only.

He was mostly concerned with the money I was making. I gave him money and told him I would see him later, which I had no intentions of doing. I went to the tourist home to see if I could salvage any clothing that was left. The place was boarded up. *All I could think of is where can I go?* I called home. My mother begged me to come home. Reluctantly, I did. I just wanted to shower and go to bed. I didn't even feel like getting high, but all that changed once I walked in my mother's place. It was filled with her friends and they were getting high, drinking, and socializing.

My mother introduced me to a few of the people, and as I made my way to what was supposed to be my bedroom, I realized that someone was occupying it. My mother pulled me to the side and informed me sbout what was taking place. She had rented the room out for a couple of hours. That was how she was getting extra cash to feed her habit. My mother told me that she was behind on the rent and asked if I could help her. I did. After all, I was staying there, not going to school and selling drugs. Her male companion seemed to be enjoying himself a lot. He just kept looking at me and smirking. I wanted to blow that smirk off his face with his gun. *I really hated that man, but what could I say or do?* That was my mom's business.

Once the crowd started clearing out, I went on the balcony to get some air and started thinking about what my next move was going to be. I needed to find employment and fast. I walked on the avenue and filled out an application at the *McDonald's*. I never really wanted to work there because all the patients from St. Elizabeth's Hospital frequented that place. Within two weeks, the hiring manager called me in for an interview, and I was hired.

One day I was working and the manager told me to take my break. I got my food, sat down, and began to eat. A patient walked over to me and asked me for some of my food. I said no. He unzipped his pants and pissed on the floor in front of me. I took my tray and smacked him with it, and then I threw it at him. The manager then told me to clock out because I was fired. *For real? I asked myself* after that patient pissed on the floor in front of me.

I was on get him back time. I knew when he worked and when he did the money drop for the bank. I gathered some of my friends along with my boyfriend and made plans to rob the manager. It was set up real nice. We drove up and parked by the *Number Eleven Boy's Club*, and watched as the manager walked out carrying two hefty bags. I walked up to him, and he didn't notice who I was due to the mask I wore. I told him to drop the bags. My boyfriend pulled up and jumped out, while two of my friends held guns on him.

Reluctantly, the manager gave up the bags, and we fled the scene. We got away with a little over five thousand dollars. There was four of us, so one thousand two hundred and twenty-five dollars a piece was good for us. We parted our ways and never spoke of that incident. Two days later, a knock came on my door and it was MPD, asking my whereabouts on the date and time of the robbery. My mother vouched that I was home, and they said that they would be in touch. They came back and asked more questions and the same answers were given. We got away with that one. My mother had her doubts about the incident, but she never spoke of it again.

*****

I began to hang out with a different crowd of people. Most of them from Barry Farms. Some were from Highland and Valley Green. Nonetheless, they were ruthless people and I gravitated to them. I hooked up with several people in the drug game and my name began ringing out on the street. I was the one people wanted to see. I was the one they wanted to purchase their drugs from. If they didn't get it directly from me, they didn't want it. As time went on, Brian and I went our separate ways. I found out I was pregnant, and I was twenty-three years old. I really didn't want a baby. I knew it would slow me down from doing what I was enjoying, which was selling drugs and getting high. I had my son, Kevin DiAndre Smith, on August 2nd, 1988.

Before my six week checkup, I was locked up on another possession and possession with the intent to distribute a controlled substance charge. I was reprimanded to DC jail. I was given a number, which was two hundred and thirty dash eight hundred and eighty-seven and a butt ugly orange jumpsuit. My picture was taken and I was sent to South One. While sitting in that jail cell, all I could think of was what was becoming of my life. I asked God to get me out that situation, and I promised I would never do that again. I needed to be home with my newborn.

The judge saw things differently. I was a menace to society. I was labeled as an unfit mother who didn't need to have children because I was unfit for the outside world. I was sentenced to twenty to sixty months, and I was to be sent to Lorton then I would be shipped off to the federal institution in Lexington, Kentucky. They had moved the men from dorms six and seven and moved the women on the hill to those two dorms. I knew a few of the girls there, but I just didn't want to get close to any of them. When we arrived to Lorton it was time for lunch. We rode down on the same bus that had brought us there. When we arrived to the chow hall, I saw my father. I yelled his name out and ran towards him. The guards began to surround us and asked us to step a part from one another.

I exclaimed, "This is my father!"

They had us go to the captain's office. He called us in the office and asked us questions on how we're related. Once that was justified, they allowed us to meet twice a week. My father was a barber, so he was already in good standards with the captain and staff at Lorton. I didn't realize how good my dad had it in there. I was sent packages, food, drugs, almost anything a person in jail or prison could want or need.

Within a month's time, I was shipped to Kentucky to do my twenty to sixty months. We were placed in shackles and handcuffs, and then we boarded a con air plane for transportation. The guards had rifles and stun guns. It all seemed like something from a movie, and I was the playing the lead role. As we were getting off the plane, they asked if any of us had been in a federal prison before and to state our number. I didn't have one, but was given one immediately once I got off the plane. The numbers given would tell an officer where you were from. My number was zero-zero-eight-six-six-zero-zero-seven. The double zero-seven meant you were from the DC area.

There was a lot of us coming off that plane. I got real familiar with the place fast, and that is where I met my girlfriend, Lady T. I was sent to a place called the *bus stop* because that's where new arrivals were placed before getting a room assigned to them. In order to get into a two person room, you basically had to be doing damn near a life sentence. They had their own TV's, stereos, refrigerators, etc. I was eventually moved to a ten person dorm. For count, we would have to stand outside our door with our ID on our top and call out our inmate number. My job assignment was the kitchen. I learned how to make jailhouse liquor (hooch), and how to make money delivering different food to the inmates. On chicken day, I would make a killing. Wasn't nothing like that barnyard pimp, hot out of the grease!

The money was used to get phone calls and commissary. My aunt and Brian would send me money, and I just let that accumulate. I wouldn't be doing the whole five years. I would be getting out on good behavior soon. That's what I believed. I started getting into fights over dumb shit. Territory was a big thing in the feds. If people disrespected your lover, stole from you, or a friend, all were grounds for a fight.

Lady T was a quiet person. She was secretive and never letting her guard down. They were sending some women from Marietta, Georgia to Kentucky and she got all fidgety. I asked her what was wrong. People had told me of a relationship she had with this girl called Pie. I wondered about that name and when we came face to face, I could see why and how she got that name. Her face was shaped like a pie. It was smashed in and round. She asked to meet with me. I thought that was no problem.

I knew I had to be on guard. I got a buddy of mine to give me a shank, and I had it neatly tucked away in the fold of my top. We met in the common area by the pool tables. When I approached her, she asked if I played pool. I said no. She tossed me a stick, and I tossed it back. Pie informed me she wasn't there for any drama, and if I was happy with Lady T then so be it. She had a friend who came with her, and she wanted to set the record straight with Lady T as well. That just threw me for a loop. The way people were talking, it was as if I was facing a bonafide killer.

I left the area, and went to see Lady T. She was in line for mail call, and I asked her if she had talked to Pie. She said no. I told her that if she wanted to be with her, I completely understood, and then I walked off. I went to work, having to do the dinner shift. I noticed that Lady T didn't come to dinner. I asked around for her but no one had seen Lady T. The alarms sounded off, and they were announcing all inmates to go to their assigned bunks. Something was wrong. When the guards came around, they motioned for me to get up and come with them. Looking dumbfounded, I followed. They bought me before the warden, and I was asked if I knew of the situation involving Lady T and Pie's girlfriend. I was at a loss for words.

Lady T had been stabbed in her stomach several times and was rushed to the infirmary to be transported to the hospital. They had placed Pie as well as her girlfriend were placed in solitary confinement pending ruling on the case. It seemed Pie had met with me, knowing her girl was going after Lady T with a shank. That would give her an alibi to where she was during that time. She was in the common area talking to me and playing pool.

Pie was released because they did have camera footage and her girlfriend would be facing more charges. The officers allowed the kitchen crew to go back to their stations to clean and get the menu ready for the breakfast crew. That night I couldn't sleep, wondering how all this was going to play out. They moved Pie back to Georgia in the middle of the night and placed my unit on lock down. So if I had any ideas of retribution, they couldn't come to light.

Three weeks later, Lady T arrived back to the compound. I watched over her like a mother hawk would do her babies. I waited on her hand and foot. We made time to just be alone. We would going to a movie, sit in the confines of my dormitory, or just walking the yard. Abruptly, my time would come to an end, and I would be on that plane ride back to DC jail to be released. After serving close to two years, (twenty-two months to be exact), I was about to be a free woman again. The year was nineteen-ninety-nine and I was more than ready to hit the streets.

I was placed on probation and was ordered to go to a treatment program. I sought out some friends when I got home. I got high and forgot all about treatment. I had lived back with my aunt for a while. I did go home to visit my son, Kevin. He was two and into everything. My adorable baby. His father was hesitant about me seeing him in the beginning. He already had another girlfriend. I wasn't mad. I was just upset that my son thought of her as momma. He was hardly ever with my mother, so he really didn't have the chance of knowing his grandmother until I was on the run.

I didn't go see my probation officer when I was scheduled, and when I did go my urine was always dirty. She had forewarned me that if my urine came up dirty one more time, I would be placed back in jail. I made a run for it. I stayed with friends who I knew would never turn me in and laid low. I would send them to the bank to get money or meet with my clientele and get my shipment of drugs that was sent to me and break them off something proper for doing it. My addiction continued to spiral and I was off to the races again. It seemed like I was now smoking more cocaine than I ever did. I was cooking up eight balls and dropping in boulders, just to hear the sound of the train. To have my ears clogged up and the feeling of paranoia was the euphoria I was looking for.

I began taking things that wasn't mine. I can remember going into my aunt's purse and stealing a hundred dollars out of it. I owed the coke man money, and I just needed to get him off my back. I stole her rings, watches, clothes, or anything that was of value. I went over to my mother's place. Knowing she wasn't home, I entered and stole her color television then made it seem like someone kicked her door in. I pawned the TV along with the rings and watches and was able to pay the dealer what I owed.

My aunt knew I was going through something, and knew I needed help. She asked me about going into treatment. I kept saying I would, but eventually my time ran out. The police caught up with me, and I was once again arrested and placed in the custody of a DC jail. I tried killing myself by taking a bunch of sleep meds. They found me passed out at count time and took me to the infirmary and then over to DC general hospital where they pumped my stomach then sent me to the psych ward in jail. It was in South three.

They kept me heavily sedated and on suicide watch. I even had a paper jumpsuit. By the time my court arraignment was set, I asked to go into a drug treatment program. I cried and boo hoo'd all over the courtroom. I was begging and pleading for them to give me a chance. I promised that I would do right. They sent a representative to see me. They were from *Second Genesis*. I had heard so much of that place. I just knew I was going on Harvard Street Northwest. That's where they get high in the alley and sneak back in. I knew I could make it there.

Unfortunately, I was sent to Second Genesis in Upper Marlboro, Maryland. It was in the woods on a long and whined road. You needed a vehicle just to get to the road. I entered the building and was told to sit on this hard bench in the hallway called the point. That was a seat where you made the decision on whether or not you were ready to be in this treatment program. The director of the program was an ornery old lady by the name of Mary Finch. She would give us her drug stories of how she shot dope with the legendary Billie Holliday. She would tell us how she had no veins left and had to cut holes in herself just to get the dope into her system. She had a nasty attitude. I hated her on the spot. Then it was time to meet the other residents.

I met them in my first encounter group. That's a group where they tear you down, and then build you up. I just never understood that group. I went through that program wearing signs for flagging (leaving stuff unattended). I was on three contracts, and on my way out the door. The only two things that kept me there was my probation officer, and not wanting to be in jail for the time I had remaining on my sentence. The program was up to two years, and I managed to complete it in nineteen months. I graduated and remained clean for a substantial amount of time.

I got pregnant in nineteen-ninety-two with twins. The guy was from the program with me. My twins were born on May 22nd, 1992. I had a boy and a girl. I named them Greta Darlene and Gregory Darnell Wills, Jr. During my pregnancy, their father had messed around on me with a coworker. He even had the audacity to bring her to a Narcotics Anonymous meeting that was held at the PG Hospital one evening. I was pissed. He kept telling me she was just a friend who needed help. *Yeah, right,* I thought to myself. I was treasurer for the group and my job was to keep track of the money and deposit it in the account after the meeting or the following day.

It was this guy's anniversary coming up in the next week, and I took the money and ran. I used the money to get high because I was upset about seeing Greg with that chick. I would show him. After getting high, I went into labor and my twins were born the day after their father's birthday, which was two weeks too soon. They were supposed to be born in June. My mother was called and I delivered two healthy nine pound babies. I vowed that Greg would never see those kids since he wanted to be out in the street with another female who he said needs help.

When I was able to leave the hospital, I went home with my mom and never thought to call Greg again. I wanted that chapter of my life wiped clean. I ran into some of the people who had graduated with me from Second Genesis, and they told Greg I had the babies then he tried to contact me. I talked to him through my mother and said I wanted nothing to do with him and I could take care of my kids by myself. He called constantly, and I ignored the calls. I had three kids to worry about and dealing with Brian had become a headache.

Even though I had a close relationship with my mother, things were beginning to get a little strained. I knew I could no longer be in the household with her. My mother wouldn't allow me to take my kids with me because of the life I was living. She cared for them and had a babysitter to watch them while she went to work or on one of her get high excursions. I met this guy who was a hustler, and we hit it off really good. We both knew how to get money, and it was our plan to take the Southeast by storm. We lived on Mellon Street Southeast, and we had a traphouse. The house we ran our drugs from was an asset to us. We supplied the owner with coke and dope, and we stayed in her place to profit from our drugs. I would be at the traphouse day and night, only going home to shower, change clothes, and eat. I would go check on my kids periodically, vowing I would get them from under my mother's roof.

*****

My drug activity increased as well as my hunger for crack cocaine. I was introduced to heroin. That had become such an ultimate high for me. I fell in love with the feeling it gave me. I began by snorting the powder. It began to leave me with such a feeling of sexuality that I could be whoever and whatever I wanted to be. Just snorting it gave me some type of power. I could do

34

whatever I wanted when I snorted that little bag.

Over a period of time, the snorting had become irritating to me and one of my boyfriend's friends showed me how to cook it up, pull it up in a syringe, then break the needle off and squirt it in my nose. It was okay for the most part. I just couldn't fathom the draining it caused. My boyfriend had some friend's over one evening, and I walked in on them shooting the dope up. I wanted a part of that.

He told me, "You should never play with the needle because it's hard to stop."

I could stop at any given time. I just wanted to feel like I was on top of the world. He gave me my first shot. He tied a rubber piece across my arm and plucked it. The veins immediately rose up. He stuck the needle in my arm and pulled the syringe back to see the blood come out and mix with the liquid. I thought I was going to pass out, watching that blood flow. As he pushed the mixture into my arm, I slowly began to sink down in my seat. He pulled back again, noting that he was giving it a kick and I felt a calm come over me.

I could hear people talking, but it was as if they were somewhere else or maybe it was me being somewhere else. I nodded out and could still hear the people talking and found myself answering them as well. My speech was a little slurred and my voice became low and sultry. I considered that my *sexy talk*. I knew I was feeling good and never wanted that high to end. I called my mother and told her I was on my way to pick my kids up. I said that they would be spending a few nights with me. She agreed.

I made it a point in my life that no matter what, I would never smoke, drink, or get high around my kids. I would not even smoke cigarettes. I would never expose them to that other side that I was living. After getting my kids, I headed to my place of residence. I cooked, cleaned, and gave them a bath then sent them in the room to watch television. My kids were obedient, but just nosey as hell. I guess they got that from me.

I was in the midst of cooking up some dope when Kevin, my oldest, walked out of the room. He stood at the door and looked at me then asked if he could sit out there with me. I explained to him that this was grown up time, and that he needed to be in the room with his brother and sister. He left then slammed the door. I never went after him. I just wanted the dope to take control of me and let me just drift off to an unknown place.

When my nod was over and done, I cleaned up the paraphernalia and put everything away, so that my kids couldn't come in contact with it. With just a few hours of rest, I had to get up to make breakfast. The kids were up at the break of dawn wanting to look at TV and play Atari games. I showered, cooked, got them dressed, and headed to my mom's. I sat with her for a while then took the kids to the zoo. We stayed out for most of the day, and I felt myself getting sluggish and in need of some dope. I began throwing up and having hot flashes. I sat my kids on the bench, telling them to sit there while I used the restroom.

I just had to get this dope in my system to feel better. I cooked it up and pulled it up in the syringe and tried to find a vein without a tie. I balled my fist up and found one. It was such a good feeling to get that dope in my system. I felt like I could venture more at the zoo. I made it out to my kids and we headed on to the bus stop to make it home. When we got home, my boyfriend had cooked, so the kids ate, bathed, and went directly to sleep. I knew the day out would tire them. For me the day had just begun.

I pulled my pipe out of hiding and cooked up some coke and smoked until I needed a shot of dope to bring me down. I had my boyfriend shoot me up and give me a kick then I was out. I don't remember too much about that evening. When I woke up it was a new day. My kids were still sleep, so I moved quietly as to not to disturb them. I made my way in the kitchen, I cooked then turned on the TV and the radio. I did that just to feel alive.

I felt as if I was moving fast, but actually I was moving in slow motion. I just wasn't feeling the activities for the day. I just wanted to sleep. My boyfriend took the kids with him, so he can go pick up his son and daughter and take them out. What a relief! I slept the day away. When I woke up it was to the laughter of kids playing. I asked my boyfriend if he could take my kids back to my mother's and he agreed. I gave him some money to give to her and I laid back down. I just wasn't feeling good.

My boyfriend informed me that I had a dope habit and I had to feed it. My bowels had broken and I vomited all over the bed. I just couldn't make it to the bathroom in time. He came in, closed the door, and cooked up two bags of dope and fed it in my veins. Once it started to circulate in my system, I began feeling much better. Not wanting the kids to see me like that, I asked him to take them home with promises of me calling them before they went to sleep. My mother wasn't there when he went over there, so he bought the kids back. I tried calling her, but the calls went unanswered. They would be with me another night.

I went outside, thinking I would make some sales out there and ran into a friend. He was skiied up off coke and tripping off the boat. He pointed a gun at me and robbed me of the coke I had. It was maybe three to four hundred dollars worth, but nonetheless, he took it. I ran in the house cursing and going off, yelling to my kids and his to get in the room and close the door. My boyfriend was told what had happened and he wanted to retaliate. He went out looking for my old childhood friend, but he had disappeared and no one was saying anything.

Two weeks passed, and then we had got word on where he was. My boyfriend told me I was to be the one to approach him and do what he did to me. I went on the avenue and saw him in the store. I walked in the store, pulled out my gun, put it to his head, and told him to empty his pockets. He realized what was going on and begged me to forgive him. He kept saying he was high and didn't realize that he had robbed me until it was too late. I had to do something that I knew I would regret later. I told him the worse thing he could do was to put a gun to someone's head and not pull the trigger. I pulled the trigger and shot him in his chest then stood over his body ready to shoot him again. I left out that store and never looked back.

A few days passed, and then the police came knocking on the door. They questioned me. They said they had an eyewitness who could place me at the scene of the crime. They asked me to come to the police station and I went. I listened and I talked. I told them that yes, I was in the store at the time of the shooting, but I had no knowledge of who the shooter may be. The security camera had already been confiscated, unbeknownst to me.

I found out later that my boyfriend had dealings with the store owner and paid him to have the tape dismantled. I was relieved. There was nothing to tie me to a crime except someone's word against mine. There was no bullet and no smoking gun. I just knew I was going to be under a microscope with the 7th District Police Department. I was back on the block of Mellon Street before anyone knew I was away. I cut back on the dope and continued smoking crack. It kept me more alert. It wasn't until later, that I would become paranoid from using. Everyone was a suspect that came across my path. My boyfriend and I had been making big moves. We had connects in New York, Baltimore, and with the Jamaicans. Mellon Street had become my kingdom. There was no competition. In fact, my boyfriend and I employed a lot of workers. We had crackhouses, stashhouses, and even a weapons house. We left no rock unturned.

One night, after getting a shipment in, I received a phone call from a guy who lived downstairs from us who we called our uncle. He was looking to purchase a key of coke from us. He said he would be around the way at around nine PM, and he would be driving a white caddy.

I told him I would meet him out front. That night just seemed so eerie. I went out the back door of our apartment and walked through the cut to get to the front.

As soon as I approached the sidewalk, I saw a white caddy coming down the street. I reached in my bag to get ready to make the transaction, and then all of a sudden a jump outs came from all over. I never saw it coming. The white caddy was a jump out as well. As I was pushed up against the car, I look up and see another white caddy going pass. Our uncle just looked at me and drove on. I put my head down in disgust. My neighbors all came out to witness the scene that was taking place.

The police said, "We know who drugs these are. Just give up your boyfriend and you can walk."

I replied, "Possession is nine-tenths of the law and since I possess it, it's mine."

I had one kilo, two ounces, two one hundred dollar packages, and some loose dimes and twenties in packages in my bag. They called me the *Queen Bee* and hauled me on to jail.

CHAPTER FOUR

After being booked and given a jumpsuit, I was sent on to jail, awaiting court in the morning. I had family members who worked at DC jail, and as soon as they heard I was in there, they couldn't wait to tell things like I told you so or I knew you'd be back. I wasn't in the mood to hear none of that shit. I went before the judge and a lot of shit was dropped, but because I had priors, I was sentenced to two to five years. I did nine months due to a technicality.

I thanked God that I was being released. My boyfriend had made sure I was taken care of as well as my kids. When I came home, I was ready to open shop back up. A couple of months had passed and a friend of ours had come over and asked if someone could drive him to North Carolina. He had a case there and had to be in court in the morning. He had just got out of a body cast and had a halo screwed on his head to keep it straight. I had asked my boyfriend if it would be okay to drive him out there, and he said it would. This guy was like family. He was like a brother. We were real tight.

I called my kids and told them I had to go out of town, and that I would see them when I get back, but my boyfriend would make sure they were okay and had all they needed while I was gone as well as my mom. I had brought some bags of coke with us as we made this trip to the boonies. We took turns driving, so that the other could smoke and sometimes we would just pull over and get high then continue on our journey.

As we got closer to North Carolina, we stopped at a gas station to fuel up, get coffee, snacks, and to smoke. He wanted to stop at his aunt's house since it was early and as we made our way there, we noticed his uncle in a truck. He talked to him for a minute and introduced me to him, and then we were on our way to see his attorney before court. His attorney informed him that he had court at one that afternoon.

With time on our hand, we decided to just ride around until it was time to be there to plead his case. We drove to a shopping center in Lincolnton, North Carolina, and he said he wanted to get his wife some shoes. I wanted something to eat and asked him if he wanted something. He said he didn't. I drove up to the McDonald's and parked the car. We both got out the car. He went towards the shoe store, and I went to McDonald's.

I can't remember all that I ordered, but it was enough if he decided he wanted something. I was in the midst of drinking my coffee when he ran up to the car and said let's go. I put my coffee down and was about to put my bag in the back seat when he kept urging me to hurry up. I couldn't figure out what the rush was for all of a sudden, but I buckled up and pulled off. As I hit the street, I noticed a police car going in and out of traffic as if they keeping tabs on the car I was driving. In less than a minute, the siren and flashing lights came on. The patrol car was now behind me, and asking me to pull over on his loudspeaker.

I was just about to do that when all of a sudden my friend's foot smashed down on the accelerator, and we went flying through the streets of Lincolnton. I didn't know where I was going. We were just flying through town clueless. We were going so fast that when the car hit the train tracks it flew up in the air. When it landed, two tires busted, and he ran from the car. I was left there in a daze, wondering what the hell had just happened.

The car was immediately surrounded by cops, and they kept asking me where did the guy go. *How was I supposed to know?* I didn't have a clue to where I was, let alone where someone else was. The officer took me out the car and asked me if I had any weapons inside. I said no. He asked where did we throw the gun. What gun I asked. He said the one used to rob those two shoe stores. *Rob? Shoe stores? What?*

He then pulled out two shoe bags from the backseat of the car and asked me what size shoe did I wear. I said a seven to seven and a half. The shoes were a size ten. He asked me to try them on. *For what? Didn't I just say what size I wore?* I thought to myself. They searched the car thoroughly. They found two crack pipes and empty bags. One of the officers said the car I was operating was stolen. I was confused. *Stolen? From where? When?*

He said a lady in DC said she went into a corner store and when she came out her car was gone. Talk about going up shit's creek with no paddle. I was heading upstream fast. The other officer's finally found my friend and bought him back to the car. He was covered in mud. He must've fell in the mud head first, trying to get away. They caught him at the top of a fence, trying to climb over. The wire was caught into his halo, so he was stuck on the fence. I had to laugh to keep from crying.

Never would I have thought I would be involved in such a mess just by taking someone to court. In fact, we missed that due to being subdued by North Carolina's finest. We were taken into custody, and I was interrogated for what seemed like hours. I was too tired to talk. I just wanted to wake up from that horrible nightmare.

When they took us to the county, and I was fingerprinted that so called dream became a reality. Here I was four and a half hours away from home. I was away from my mom, my kids, and my boyfriend. I would have given anything to make that go away. They sent us different ways and all I wanted to do was sleep. All I did was cry. In the cell there was only me and another female. She was drunk and didn't even know I was in there until in the morning when all she wanted to know if I was eating. The food looked good. They had a cook who has been there for years, and she was a bonafide Southern chef. She was a Caucasian older lady who was maybe in her late sixties. She was plump with a cherub face and dimples.

She made it her business to greet the prisoners each morning and ask for requests on the food we may wanted. *Really?* This was like a Southern *Hilton Hotel*. Breakfast was pancakes, sausage, oatmeal, juice, and coffee. I just settled for the coffee. That other prisoner could eat the food. I didn't trust it. I stayed in the county jail for nine months, waiting for this case to go to trial.

During my stay at Lincolnton County Jail, my friend had been trying to contact me and find out what was going on with the case. The jailers were real nice. They had 1 black female jailer and one black male jailer. The black female jailer would tell me how Lincolnton really was. She said in her apartment complex they had a sign that read: *NO NIGGERS ALLOWED! WILL BE SHOT!* She said they had burned crosses in front of her building, but she wasn't going to allow them to run her away. She was a nice lady.

I discovered from her that my friend took his halo off, so he wouldn't be recognized by the victims of the store. I met with an attorney, who really did nothing for my case. I had already called home and informed them that I would probably get some time. Not knowing how much, I was just waiting to see. My boyfriend kept my account pumped, so I wanted for nothing while I was in there. We talked on a regular and when my kids came over I use to tell them I was away at school and would see them real soon.

The day came to find out my fate. I spoke honestly about the events that took place, and my friend only watched. The judge asked the victims what was my involvement, and they stated there was no female involved in the robbery of either shoe store. As the judge was talking, it dawned on me that my friend had robbed two shoe stores. One was called *Pic & Pay* and the other one was called *Shoe Show*.

I couldn't understand why he committed a robbery. He had money and could buy whatever he wanted. They kept asking about a gun. No gun was recovered and one of the victims said he just said he had a gun but never presented one. Okay, that was an iffy situation. *If there was no gun, robbery with a dangerous weapon would be dropped to two counts of robbery for him, but what would be my outcome?*

I wasn't anywhere near the stores. They checked my story out. The police went to the McDonald's where I said I had purchased food. The receipt and food was in the bag in the backseat, and they also went to look at the cameras in that timeframe. I was looking at freedom. So I thought. The judge asked my friend what was my involvement, and he just looked at me. I pleaded for him to say something, and no words ever came out his mouth. I was defeated. I cried in that courtroom.

The judge asked me how did I plead, and I said not guilty. After going over his notes and asking me to stand along with my fake ass attorney, the judge charged me with accessory after the fact and aiding and abetting to two counts of robbery. I was sentenced to thirteen years, one month, and twenty-five days, and then I was to be sent to the *North Carolina Correctional Institute for Women* (NCCIW) at 1034 Bragg Street, Raleigh, North Carolina.

*****

By the time I left the court building and got back to the county jail, the bus was almost there to pick me up. I tried calling out but they had turned the phones off. One of the jailers allowed me to make a call from the office to alert my boyfriend of what went on, where I was going, and for how long. He was devastated, and I was too.

How was I supposed to do all this time for something I didn't do or know anything about. As I walked to change my clothes, I got a glimpse of my friend, who had now become public enemy number one. He looked at me with pain in his eyes, hung his head down, and then walked away with a jailer by his side.

The ride wasn't too long. I was numb when I arrived at what would be my home for the next thirteen years. I just went through the motions of squatting, coughing, showering, and getting a doo doo brown dress to wear. After being fingerprinted, I was given a number: zero-zero-five-three-eight-seven-zero-six. That would become my state number. A number I would always be known by in that facility.

There was quite a few of us being processed and once we were done, we headed over to the infirmary to get checked out and then we were sent to a place called reception. That's where we remained until we took all types of tests, got medically cleared, and found out what dorm we would be assigned to.

This prison housed minimum custody, medium custody, close custody, lifers, and death row inmates. I even met the *Black Widower* while I was there. She was an amazing lady. She spoke of her crimes, but insisted she was innocent. I figured she could be innocent because hell I was. I wasn't there to judge anyone. After about three weeks, I made my way down the hill to the Falcon Unit, Dorm K. There were thirty-four beds in each section. There was sections KA, KB, KC (dining room dorm), and KD. The other side of Falcon was Dorm L. There was the Phoenix Unit. Cardinal was for long termers and lifers. Eagle was medical and lock down.

The dining room was immaculate. The food was good and plenty. That would be my first job. I would learn that on chicken and pork chop day, you could get paid to bring it out of the dining room. Not only that, but you could get paid for produce as well. Onions were a commodity. I made most my money in stealing from the dining room, until I was able to get money in from the outside. I had a lot of different jobs in my ten years of incarceration. I worked on the yard, in the laundry, in the canteen, in the dental lab, on the third shift cleaning crew, and in travel and tourism. I even joined the step team to keep myself occupied.

I never received my diploma or G.E.D., but I attended college classes and even did independent courses through the mail. I tried to get into any and everything that would help me get out of prison early. I was even on the step team called the S.W.A. (Steppers With Attitudes), which I definitely had.

*****

One evening, I sat in my dorm and decided to write my mother. All I knew is that she had moved back to Palmer Park with my aunt, and I really didn't want them to know my whereabouts. My kids were with my boyfriend, and I had doubts about allowing them to come see me in prison. I wrote a long letter to my mother, and told her all that went on and how I ended up in North Carolina's Women Prison. I begged her not to tell the family where I was. I just didn't want to hear the I told you so's, stuff about the choice of friends I made, along with all the other bullshit that came with it.

Two weeks later, I received a letter from my aunt, asking me if it would be okay if they come to see me and could I put them on my visitation list. I was upset. *Why did my mother tell them?* I thought to myself. *If I put them on my list were they going to come down and harass me, and tell me how stupid I was to be doing dumb shit with any and everybody? Would they ask me when was I going to get myself and my life together because I was getting too old for all this shit?*

In the letter my aunt asked me to call her and I did. I agreed to them coming to see me and with that, my aunt sent me some money. It was a hot day in July when my family made it to visitation. Visitation was held in the auditorium where it was spacious and the officers could walk around freely to make sure no contraband was being passed amongst the inmates and that none was going out. After being searched going in, I saw my two aunts, my cousin, and her new baby. I immediately made my way to them. We hugged and gave out kisses, and then I had a chance to hold my baby cousin. He was a beautiful little baby, and I just didn't want to let him go. I was missing my kids so much that I gravitated to him, as if he was mine and he would remain behind those walls with me as I did my bid.

The talking went smooth. It was nothing like I had planned in my head, but civilized. As time moved on, one of my aunt's said there was something they needed to talk to me about. My cousin asked for her baby, and I was reluctant to give him to her. She kept saying that it was time to feed him, and then I was like take your damn baby. I was in my feelings.

My aunt pulled a paper from her pocket and was about to passed it to me, but one of the guards intercepted it. She informed my family that nothing could be passed amongst the visitor's and inmates. The officer asked my aunt what was on the paper and my aunt kind of leaned towards the officer to tell her. I was unaware of what was about to take place next.

My aunt gently said, "Sherita, your mother passed away in October of nineteen-ninety-six."

That was nine months ago. That was in July when I first came to prison. Now things were beginning to make sense. I never received a response from my mother because she never received my letter. When the letter arrived to my aunt's house, she was already gone.

When my aunt wrote me, her letter on read: *Your mother is no longer here with me.*

I took that as saying that my mother had moved on, not that she was dead. My head began to swirl and it got extremely quiet in that auditorium. It was as if everyone knew what was happening before I did. I cried and cried, and the officers ended my visit and escorted me directly to my dorm. My mother was gone, I was in prison for ten years, and I couldn't see my kids. *What am I going to do now?* I thought to myself.

My mother was cremated. They family told me she was at peace when she passed from brain cancer. It ate from the inside out. It was good to know that my father had been by her bedside the whole time. I felt guilty because I was not being there for my mom at her time of need. I should've been there for her. She had always been there for me. *How could I let this happen?* I questioned to myself.

I cried until I was sick. I was rushed to the infirmary and was admitted. I took a bunch of pills while being there because I just wanted my life to end. They rushed me to *Wake Med Hospital*, where my stomach was pumped. I remained in their care for three days and when I was released, I was sent back to the infirmary on suicide watch. They placed me in paper scrubs and took all my clothing and pens out the room.

A psychiatrist came to see me, and I was in no mood to talk to anyone. Talking wouldn't bring my mother back. The only thing I could do was rock back and forth then cry. I was put on several mental health medications, and I didn't know whether I was coming or going. They kept me on halidol, seroquil, and doxepin to get me to sleep and be stable at night. I was on paxil, Prozac, and caffergot to get me moving in the morning. I was drugged up and couldn't do a lot on my own.

The psychiatrist would have a nurse on standby and document my every move. I was a walking zombie. When I wasn't asleep, I was staring into space while mumbling some type of shit. I was incoherant. I begged the nurse to let me go back to my dorm.

After a month had passed, I was able to go back to population and try to get on with my life. It wasn't easy, but I maintained for a while. I got into many fights and was sent to single cell for fifteen days or more each time. I was a loose cannon. I had become an animal, and the only way to tame a wild animal is to keep it caged. That's how I spent most of my time in NCCIW. The solitude was great. I was just missing the cigarettes. When people got locked up to come to a single cell, they would *suitcase* cigarettes and we would pay an extraordinary price just to get that taste of nicotine.

Once I was released from single cell and able to go back to the compound, I found other things to get into like selling drugs. The officers were bringing all sorts of drugs in, and I had friends I had hooked up with who had alliances with the top officers. I began by selling weed. I would roll the joints and sell them for two dollars, and then came the crack epidemic. You could sell a small piece of crack and get forty dollars for it because the inmates were fiending for their past time vices. I never got high while doing time. It wasn't on my mind. I was only concerned with making money and not get caught while doing so.

I had come in my dorm one afternoon after working all day in the kitchen, and I noticed we were having a shakedown in our dorm. They even had the dogs come out. I had left the weed in my locker tucked away in a jar in the back. There was no way I was going to be able to retrieve it due to all the officers in the dorm and the dogs sniffing around. When they came to my locker, I was told to open it, step away, and follow the officer to the bathroom to be stripped searched. By the time I was searched, I was placed in handcuffs and told they had found fifty marijuana joints in my locker. I wasn't shocked.

They wanted to know who I had got it from because they knew I didn't receive visitors. I never said anything. I lived by the street code. If you have it, it's yours. The person I was selling it for looked out for me. I had money sent to my account, and I was still able to order commissary while being locked in single cell again.

I kind of enjoyed being locked down. I would sleep all day then go outside for recreation. I would shower, and then go back to the confines of my own personal space. That was how I did my time, and that was the way I enjoyed it. Time seemed to go by fast, and when I looked up it was time for my release.

CHAPTER FIVE

I was released on March 22nd, 2006, and I remained in Raleigh. I had a girlfriend who was still locked up but would be released soon and come home with me. I was placed on probation for a short while, and I found a job really fast. I lived in a rooming house for the time being, and was saving money for an apartment. My job was as a housekeeper in a facility for elderly folks.

When my girlfriend came home in April, she also got a job there but as a C.N.A. She also got a room there, but most times we shared each other's room. We had been working for about a year when an incident involving another worker hit the news. The young lady had been stealing credit cards and wiping the elderly people out. The company that hired us knew we were felons and gave us a chance, but when that happened all the C.N.A.'s were asked to leave. My job was secured. I just didn't realize how the loss of a job would change the course of both our lives forever.

I had come home and my girlfriend was sitting in the living room with some guy. There was crack on the table and two glass stems.

The first thing that said was, "Please tell her that I didn't trick!"

That seemed odd, but I listened to her go on and on and on about whether she was soliciting sex for crack rocks or not. She was really upset and still crying, and I didn't know what to make of that. I didn't want to use, but she begged me to take a hit. I thought to myself, *What would one hit of crack do?* It did the obvious. It made me want more. During just that short time, I had forgot about being on probation and that my P.O. did random visits and took urine. If I came up dirty, I would be in violation and sent back to prison.

My girlfriend had given me the name of someone who gives up clean urine for a small fee. I met with her and got three maybe four bottles. I smoked with my girl and her friend then realized I really missed this feeling. I was paranoid for a minute or two, looking out the window and thinking every small white car was that of my P.O.

I had to get away for a minute. I went outside and called a friend and asked for some help. That was not what I was looking forward to doing. Relapsing, after being away from the drugs for so long was not a part of my plan. I knew that if I didn't smoke with her, she would think I was against her. I knew that I wanted to keep my apartment, but I couldn't afford it on just my salary.

I gave my girlfriend an ultimatum. She would have to leave the drugs alone and get some help or she would have to get out. None of that happened. We were doing drugs every day, and I was still looking for my P.O. to come at any given day and time. Eventually, I lost my job because I couldn't get there. I had spent my rent, transportation, and groceries money on crack. I kept giving my landlord a song and a dance about the rent until eventually I was summons to court and placed on the eviction list.

Two weeks later, we were on the streets. I called several people who allowed me to be at their residence until I could find another place. My girlfriend was running the streets harder than ever. She would come back with an abundance of drugs and drinks then we would get high wherever we could. Most times it was in the woods. We would just sit on logs and smoke until nightfall. We would visit various crackhouses and end up falling asleep there.

When we got up, we talked about making some power moves to get high that day. I found a job at a hotel paying a little more than the old housekeeping job, and I was glad to get back to working. I rented a room at this boarding house and allowed my girlfriend to stay with me over night but she had to leave out in the morning when I did, as to not disturb the other tenants in the house. They were nosey as hell. They were always trying to see who was in the house and who you had with you.

The landlord knew my girlfriend was staying with me some nights and charged me a little extra. We had agreed on a price to let her stay and I paid her. Within a month's time, my girlfriend and I had moved to another apartment. It was rent controlled and spacious. I could pay the rent alone and still have money to purchase crack and drinks. My girlfriend had a way of ripping people off, so she helped out with the rent and groceries.

Within a month's time, she would be missing in action for two to three days. Sometimes she would be missing for more days than that. I would go on the block and inquire about her, and people would tell me of her last movement. One day, I was on my way to the store when a friend of ours stopped me and told me I could find her in the shed of this Mexican's house. I walked to the shed and opened the door, and to my surprise my girlfriend was on her knees giving this Mexican some head. I went completely off on her and him.

She was begging me to come back, but I ignored her pleas and went back to my safe place and got high. She came to the apartment, asking to speak to me and I acted as if I wasn't there. I did manage to call her later, and I told her that her belongings would be by the door and she should come get them.

She cried begged and pleaded for me to forgive her, and eventually I did. I just knew we would never be able to sleep together anymore. She has lost my trust. We were living like roommates. My cousin had phoned me, letting me know that they were going to stop by on their way home from Myrtle Beach, South Carolina. I welcomed their visit. My aunt and cousins were introduced to my girlfriend and immediately my aunt told me she didn't like her. My aunt said that my girlfriend seemed sneaky. I didn't pay it any attention.

I talked to my family for a bit. My cousin had left me some money and as soon as they left, I ran up the block to get some crack. I had to work later that evening, but called in sick. I just wanted to stay home and get high and drink. Many of my friends had come by that day bearing gifts of crack and alcoholic beverages. I knew this was going to be an all-night event.

As morning creeped in, I called my job and told them that I had death in my family ,and that I would be leaving to go to DC within the hour. One lie led to another and by the time I went back to work they fired me. I already knew it was coming. I thought I had that shit under control, but actually the getting high and drinking had become a major part of my life. I really thought I could stop whenever I wanted to.

A convention was being held at the convention center, and me and my girlfriend decided we were going. No one knew what we were doing, so it made it real easy to celebrate fourteen years of recovery. I was living a lie. It's not like I was going to stand up and say that me and my girlfriend have been getting high all night, but I still am going to claim fourteen years of recovery. *Where they do that at?* I asked myself and the answer was nowhere that I knew of.

After we left the convention, we met with the boys on the block who let us sell packages and we were able to get money and stay high. After three months of paper chasing, we lost the apartment and I got locked up on a violation of my probation and my urine was dirty. I did six months and that gave me the courage to break it off with my girlfriend.

By the time I came home, I really had nowhere to go. *I had to find a place to lay my head, but where?* I questioned to myself. I ran into one of the dope boys, and he said he could help me out. If I stayed and ran the crackhouse I would make money, have a place to stay, and still be able to get high. That sounded like a winner to me.

The day would be filled up with people getting high off crack in one room and in another room was where they shot dope. I didn't go in that room for at least two weeks, since I had been placed there to work. I would peep in regularly just to see who was there, and I wondered if the dope was any good. I would find that out in my third week of being there.

The guy I was selling crack for also sold dope. I asked him about me selling that as well and he gave me a try. I wanted that old familiar feeling back in my life. I sat in the front room where I was stationed to be and shot my dope then I nodded off lightly. I could hear the murmurs of voices coming from the next room and the laughter from some woman sitting at the table telling jokes to her friend. I was in some place far away with no cares in the world. I was feeling as if I was floating on a cloud, and not ever wanting to come down.

Night fall had come, and the guy I was hustling for made his appearance. I was picking up money and dropping off packages like clockwork. I sat there thinking of a way to rob him of his money and drugs. He always kept a lot of money and product on him and in his vehicle. He had about seventeen different traphouses, and he would collect by himself.

I called this one guy I knew that could pull this off. He was a member of the street gang called the Bloods, and I was down with them and the Bloodettes. I use to tell people I was a Blood just to be part of the clique. I would throw up gang signs and say that I represented Deuce Trey. I would always be down for whatever they did or planned to do. I knew that once I had the Bloods in my corner that I wouldn't be touched.

I had to show them that I was about the street life. I use to carry a 9 mm with me wherever I went and dared anyone to jump out there. I met up with the guy and gave him the details of what to look for, the truck the guy drove, and when he was to be expected to be at the trap house that I worked in. We put the plan into action.

After scoping out the place for three days, my friend made his debut on the fourth day. He busted in the door then lined people up against the wall, and that was just the beginning. Never had I imagined that the dude I was working for would try to play hero. He jumped out at my friend and got pistol whipped, tied up, and gagged. That was a one man show and it was perfectly planned.

The truck alone had over ten thousand dollars in it, and my bossman had five thousand dollars in his pockets. He had on three gold chains, rings that were diamond studded, and a nice Rolex watch. All that would be pawned. Seventy-five hundred dollars a piece was looking to be real good.

My friend, good to his word, put my money up for me and I was ready to pay a visit to the other houses. The guy I worked for never knew what hit him, and he never knew it was me who had him set up to be robbed. He never knew the other houses were going to be hit, so we didn't linger too much at this house.

He finally got someone to ride with him for protection, and he asked about stepping someone up to be at the house I worked. I told him it would be great to have muscles in the house in the event that something like this happened again. Two weeks later, five more of his houses were hit and he began questioning people's loyalty to him. I thought he had an idea that I was involved because of the questions he asked, but I never gave in. I just knew this was the beginning of many more to come.

I went and opened a bank account. I had to keep that lump sum of money somewhere besides in a duffel bag in the closet for anyone to be able to get. Later that evening, my friend from the Bloods came through and told me he hit the other houses. Three came up with cash and drugs and the last two had only drugs. We agreed to split it all up. I was coming up and no one knew the things I was doing to get there. They only knew me as being a crackhead and a dopefiend. I would soon show them.

I took the money he had given me and banked it. The drugs I kept in a locked safe box at my friend's house. I paid her for allowing me to stash drugs there and gave her a package for herself to do as she pleased. Months went by and no one suspected me. I went through my day doing what I do, and never to raised an eyebrow from anyone.

One day I stepped out the house and saw the police everywhere. As the crowd grew deeper, I walked up to the corner to get a better look. Two people had been robbed and shot on the corner of State Street. I heard the whispers of it being drug-related. What I wasn't prepared to hear was the names that rang out of their mouths. *Was it really my boy who had got shot? Who shot him and why? Was he in the middle of a war or did he get caught doing something?* I asked to myself as a lot of questions flooded my head.

Once the ambulance arrived, I was able to get a good look at both of them. It was my dealer, the guy I worked for, and some dude from Bloodworth Street. No drugs were found on the scene and the car keys that belonged to my dealer were given to me by his friend, and I was then given instructions on what to do. He had a duffle bag full of crack, which was broken down to different size packages. I was to deliver the packages to the addresses on the sticky note and collect the money. His friend would be riding with me and handling the money, and being the guys eyes and ears while he was in the hospital. I assigned a friend of mine to oversee the traphouse, while I was making that power move for my dealer.

The ride to all those houses had me tired and ready to eat. We stopped at the Chinese place and got something to eat, while we were out then headed back to my traphouse. Everything had been sold and I took the liberty of getting what I needed out the truck to last throughout the night and into the wee hours of the morning. Two days later, my dealer was released and promised that things were going to get better and security was going to get tighter.

I told him I had saved up little money and was looking for a place to move. I wanted a place to lay my head, and to still be able to run the traphouse. I looked around the area and the only place I could find was on Garner Road. *I really didn't want to be there, but with not many options where else was it to go*, I said to myself.

I walked back to the boarding house and rented a room. I was dealing with this young guy who sold drugs, and as long as he could keep my habit up we stayed together. I got pregnant and two months later the police raided the boarding house. I got locked up again. I had a warrant out for my arrest and it finally caught up to me.

I served fourteen months and had my babies while being incarcerated. I had twins again. I had two boys named Khalil Arman and Khalyle Armani. They were born prematurely, and I had their grandmother pick them up from the hospital once they gained enough weight to leave. Their father and I knew weren't going to be together when I came home because he was sleeping with everybody, and I just couldn't have that in my life anymore.

My time in prison went by fast and before I knew it, I was home. I met this guy named Jeffrey, but his friends called him Shymeed. He was a Sunni Muslim and at that time so was I. I just didn't practice the religion nor attend any services since I left prison. Shymeed and I got along really good. That's how it usually is in the beginning of a relationship. He took me out to a nice place and we shared our life stories with one another. He told me he sold drugs and I told him I did as well. I moved in with him and we were not only lovers, but partners as well.

Moving in with Shymeed was out of convenience. I had nowhere to go. We married in a couple of months and that's when all hell broke loose. He started beating me because of his jealousy of other people, but I stayed in the relationship. I used the money that I banked to help pay the rent and keep up my appearance as well as his. He wasn't a big time dealer as he made himself out to be. It was my money that afforded him to deal with the local dealers and a few who were from out of town.

He would send me out to meet the dealers and make the transactions, and when I returned he would smell me as if I were out screwing then beat me. He took my bank card and got my money out, and I was only left with the pain he embarked on me. I would take my crack and dope and go into the closet then smoke and shoot up just to escape the feelings I was left to deal with. Shymeed beat me so bad one day that I was admitted into *Wake Medical Hospital*, and I was there for two weeks.

Shymeed came to visit and promised me he would never do it again, and he kept telling me how much he loved me and how blessed he was to have me in his life. The doctor's had told me beforehand that my ribs were bruised, and that I had suffered a concussion that caused me to black out. They asked who did this do me and I said some guys had jumped me, never once placing blame on Shymeed.

I called my Muslim instructor that I had met while being in NCCIW, and she told me of a friend of hers that had a safe house in Goldsboro, North Carolina, and that I would have to be clean to get in there. I explained to her that I needed to get away from my husband before he killed me, and that I was still on drugs. She said that she would get back in touch with me. A week after I got released from the hospital, Shymeed had put his hands on me again. He got on top of me and began to strangle me.

He looked me in my face, and said, "Die bitch! Die!"

Then Shymeed spit in my face. At that moment, when I looked in his face I saw the Devil himself. The man I pledged my love to actually wants me dead. I had always said that when someone spits in your face it's over. There's no coming back from that.

A knock had come on the door and that allowed me to escape his wrath. I ran up the street to the phone booth and called the police. They asked me to wait right there, and when they pulled up Shymeed was walking up the street towards me.

I was telling the police what had transpired, and then Jeffrey said, "Tell them you did that to yourself."

The police was wondering how, and then they noticed my neck had whips and scratches on it and I was bleeding. They knew I couldn't have done that to myself and immediately locked Shymeed up. I called my Muslim instructor the next morning, and she asked me to meet her at her school. I was there before two PM, and her friend arrived and took me back with her to Goldsboro, where I would be starting a new life. It was a transitional program, and I was ready to start over.

*****

There was only three of us there and one young lady had a baby. I went job searching and got lucky. I was hired to work at *K & W Cafeteria* in the *Berkeley Mall*. It was a great experience. I started on the front line, and then the regional vice president asked me about being a baker. I didn't know nothing about making homemade breads and desserts. He asked me how did I make cornbread and I told him that I buy Jiffy Cornbread mix. I explained that I crack an egg, add milk, beat, add sugar, and butter. Then I grease my pan and viola, and freshly baked cornbread. He laughed.

The regional vice president took his suit jacket off, rolled up his sleeves, pulled out the recipe card, and then he got down and dirty to show me how to make rolls, cornbread, and Mexican cornbread. I became a big hit there. I began to learn different stations, and I knew I would work my way to management real fast.

As I was in the dining area helping a waitress clean her tables, who did I run into? It was Shymeed mother. She tried to make conversation with me. His mother asked me why didn't I tell her I had her son locked up. I asked her why didn't she tell me he beats his women. She looked shocked and said she didn't know that he was back to doing that. I told her look lady he never stopped.

She couldn't wait to get back to Raleigh, and tell her psycho son that she had seen me and where. Shymeed got released from jail only because I never made it back to Raleigh to testify against him. Shymeed made his way to Goldsboro and threatened to kill me, and he also told my manager's that he would kill them if they stood in his way. My manager called the police, and Shymeed was taken into custody. He had violated his probation by leaving without his P.O.'s permission, and he also had a gun in his possession.

I was asked to come to Raleigh by the court system, and my manager said he would take me because he also had to testify against him. I felt a sense of relief that it would all be over. On the day we get to the courthouse, I found out that Shymeed was a bigamist. His marriage to his first wife still wasn't over. He had the assumption that she had already signed the papers, and she hadn't. Therefore, we weren't really married. I would had to go to the courts and fight the marriage in order to get it annulled. I just wanted to be rid of him for good. Shymeed was to serve nine months in jail and I was free from him.

*****

I went home and got on the computer then looked on Facebook. I saw so many old, but familiar faces. I saw a picture of this young lady who favored me so much. I sent her a friend request and told her she looked like my sister and asked if she was to give me a call. Within the hour, she called me crying and boo hooing and I was also. We finally were able to connect after all those years. She told me she had a son and I told her I had kids as well. We vowed to keep in touch.

My job at K & W was going great, and I was soon able to get my own house. A friend I had known in prison had some people she knew who rented out houses for cheap. I had a one level, three bedroom house. It had a large living, dining room, and great kitchen space. I also had a car port and French doors that opened to what I called a *bachelor's pad*. When you entered the French doors there was a spacious living room. There was a door that opened to a long hallway that had a kitchen at the end, and to the right was the bedroom and bathroom.

That was a lot of space for just me, so I decided I would rent out a room. I didn't want just anyone living with me and besides that, I had a place off the carport that someone could rent. I finally rented it after a month of being there, and I charged them five hundred dollars a month for rent and they paid half of the electric. They agreed and I had a tenant.

After a couple of months, my tenant got arrested for indecent exposure, possession of drugs, and possession of drug paraphernalia. He was raising pure hell out in the middle of the driveway. I felt sorry for him. I knew he wouldn't get jail time because he was mentally ill, which they would soon find out.

I went back inside the house to prepare for work in the morning. When I arrived at work, the regional vice president was there and asked to speak to me. He asked if I could be stationed in Raleigh as a baker and lead vegetable cook, and he would pay my hotel expenses until I found suitable living arrangements. I agreed, and I would be off to Raleigh within a month's time. My tenant was being held in the psych ward, so I asked his caregiver to come collect his belongings.

I called my landlord to tell him of my moving to Raleigh by the end of the month. He was okay with it and told me if ever I decide to come back to Goldsboro that he would look out for me. I would be forever grateful to him and his wife for giving me a chance to rent a home from them. I cleaned the house, packed my belongings, and my friend drove me to Raleigh.

I went to the boarding house and luckily they had a couple of rooms available. I chose the one with a kitchenette, so I didn't have to be around a lot of people. Going back to work in Raleigh was going to be challenging. I knew that I would eventually run into Shymeed in a few months, and I really didn't want to see him because I knew it would only be trouble. When I first got to Raleigh he still had six more months left on his sentence, and I know he was a raging bull inside the prison.

I saw his mother a couple of times and she asked me to go to the courthouse and speak with the A.D.A. and help them overturn his sentence. *Did she really think I was boo boo the fool?* Hell, he was no longer my problem. We're not even married. It would take a lifetime for me to regain my maiden name back, but eventually I would get it. I worked long hours and came home dead tired only to get a few hours of sleep and have to return to work the next day at seven AM.

I threw myself into my job. I would call my twins dad and have him to bring the kids over for me to see them and spend some time with them. I would usually do that on a Saturday when I was off. I would lay around and call my sister just to say hey, and I love you. I was put in touch with my stepmom and was able to speak to my brother. My father had relations outside his marriage and bore two children. He had a son and a daughter. His relationship with my brother's mom was a little different. When I was in my addiction, she would allow me to stay there with her and her other children. Therefore, I always called them my brothers and sisters, and they looked up to me as their oldest sister. We had a bond that could never be broken.

In total, there is nine of us. There was four boys and five girls. I would never think of them as anything else. I loved each and every one of them unconditionally and equally. I would go out on a limb for my siblings.

Around the end of October to early November, my sister and I had talked about me coming back home. She had told me that our father wasn't doing too well, and it would be good for me to be back home. My sister said I would be staying with her and her family, after all, she was a married woman now with a son, and she said she had an extra room I could use. After I made arrangements with her, I informed my manager I would be leaving by the end of November. I told him that I would be willing to train someone for my position, so that he knows it would be done correctly and accurately.

I came in early and stayed late to get this young lady trained, and she was doing a terrific job. I was quite proud of myself. I got home and called my sister then gave her a date. It was finalized. I would be coming back home within two weeks. I primped and prepped myself, awaiting for my sister's arrival. When the car pulled up, she got out and came to the door. We looked at each other, hugged and cried. I met her husband and for the first time, and I met my nephew.

He was her all over again. He seemed thrilled to know he had an aunt who was in North Carolina and would be moving in with them. I didn't have to pay my sister anything, but I made sure I helped her when needed around the house. We made a trip to see my *stepmom*, and she was ecstatic. She couldn't believe how much my sister and I looked alike. Both of our hair was done in a short style. My sister's hair was black and mine was more of an auburn color. Nonetheless, we were Billy's kids!

Billy could never deny any of his children. In fact, our brother looked so much like our dad that it was scary. He even has his hands and nails. He was tall, dark, and handsome. Yep, he was just like our daddy. The only thing that sets them apart was that my brother wasn't bowlegged like my father, but he was Billy reincarnated. Being at my sister's house was great because it would afford me the opportunity to see what I'd missed in the sixteen years I'd been away. So, much had changed that I couldn't believe it. It felt as if I was a tourist visiting an unknown place.

I would get up in the mornings and go to *Iverson Mall* then window shop. I was mentally thinking of what I would get and when I would get it. I had to stop and get me the famous Snickerdoodle cookies. My word, they are to die for! I would walk over to Marlow Heights Shopping Center, which was next door and put in applications where I heard they were hiring. I also walked further down the street to the *Family Dollar* and the furniture store and put in applications there as well.

It was still early so I caught the P-Six going to *Eastover Shopping Center*, so I could begin my sightseeing tour of DC. I stopped and bought some cigarettes from the tobacco store and walked across the street to wait for the A-Six or A-Eight to get to Martin Luther King Jr. Avenue. I reached my destination, so I rung the bell and got off.

I stood in front of *Popeye's* and just looked across the street to the park to see if I saw some familiar faces. I took my chances and went over there. I ran into quite a few people that I grew up with and began to reminisce over the good old days. They offered me drinks of Hennessey, Vodka, 211 beer, and the most famous drink of them all, Velicoff. I even saw a few people drinking Mad Dog 20/20 and Cisco. It was unbelievable.

I sat there for a while and played cards, smoked cigarettes, and talked shit. I was ready to make my way home and a friend of mine from so long ago offered me a ride since she lived over in the area which I was going. I got home, went outside to smoke a cigarette then chill with my furry nephew. He was so cute. He was a shih tsu who was full of life and spoiled to the core. I vowed that when I moved into my place I would get me a furry friend.

My brother-in-law made his way in. He was ready to prepare dinner, and I was ready to go take a shower. When I was done, I made my way down to the basement where I got on the computer to play some games and wait for my sister and nephew to get in. Me and my fur ball nephew played fetch and catch then after he got bored with that, he just wanted me to rub his belly so he could rest. I always said that dog's had the best life, and if I was to ever be reincarnated please let me come back as a puppy.

My nephew came rushing downstairs and we played our favorite game, Deal or No Deal. Then he showed me how to play bowling on the Wii. I really couldn't get the hang of it, so I sat down and watched him. He put on a fitness tape and we danced around like crazy, doing all the impossible moves those people were trained to do.

I was tired and decided to go on to bed. I wasn't hungry, but I did have some chips to snack on once I took my meds. I woke up the next morning feeling refreshed and waited for my nephew to come out the bathroom so I could wash my face, brush my teeth, and eat a bowl of cereal. When my nephew headed off to school, my sister and brother-in-law headed out as well. I went down the basement, got on the computer and began sending out my resume and cover letter to various businesses.

Once I was done, I showered and headed out the door. I decided I would go see my son's grandmother who lived in Barry Farms. I got on the bus, plugged my earpiece and listened to music all the way to my destination. Once I reached my stop, I got off across the street from *Birney Elementary School* and walked across the street. I ran into Brian's brother. We talked a bit and he told me that Brian is in prison doing twenty to life. I asked him about his mother, and he said that she was well and in the house. We walked down there together. Ms. Teresa looked charmingly well for her age. She was still full of life, love, and laughter at the age of seventy-one. Ms. Teresa still got around by driving her own car and refused to allow anyone to stagnate her or stand in her way. She was a beautiful woman. Ms. Teresa was just feisty as hell and would curse you out in a hot New York minute and still be alright with you.

Ms. Teresa and I talked about Brian, and then we changed the subject to Kevin. She said she missed her only grandson and wanted him to come back from *Niagara Falls University*. Kevin did random visits to see his father but suddenly withdrew from seeing him. I believe Kevin just couldn't deal with the thought of both his parents leaving him and not being there for him in his time of need. My son was a loner. Kevin never wanted to be around anyone except family, but especially his brother and sister. The twins were four years younger than Kevin, but he enjoyed spending every waking moment with them. He would always tell me mommie, they're my babies. I would reply okay, sweetie, they're yours. He never wanted to be apart from them, but due to circumstances beyond anyone's control, they were separated from each other, but had visited quite often. Now that my mother was gone, they really had no one to be there for them.

I left, feeling bad. Not being able to be there for my kids really began to hit me. I walked up to the recreation center to play a game of pool and some ping pong then that's when I met Tyrone. I really wasn't looking for a relationship, and he was all up in my face like a washcloth. He was a medium built redbone dude. I wasn't feeling that. I had this notion that all redboned guys were conceited and stuck on themselves. That's how Brian had portrayed himself to be, like he was God's gift to women. *Yeah right,* I thought to myself. Being a beater and manipulator was more of his steelow. He earned that and lived up to it.

Tyrone was a real charmer. He was a sweet talker. Tyrone would tell the ladies what he thought they wanted to hear, and he would be grinning all the while. I played him in a game of pool and he tried to get all up on me from behind.

I yelled, "Excuse me, but you're a tad bit too close."

He replied, "I apologize, ma."

I stated, "I'm not your, ma. My name is Sherita."

He was enjoying that because I could see him with a sly smirk on his face. He asked me if I was seeing anyone, and I told him no. I really was not looking for anyone. Tyrone told that he wanted to get to know me, and he wanted to know if he gave me his number would I call. I said maybe one day. He gave his phone number to me, and then I walked out the door to go home.

I decided not to go around that way for a while. I focused more on getting a job. Free time would come soon enough. I was on my phone, and I noticed that I had two emails. I looked at the emails and had two job offers. I had one from *Steak in the Sack* and the other was for *Giant*. Both were in the Marlow Heights Shopping Center, and I would be able to work both. Steak in the Sack needed me from seven AM to three PM, and Giant would want me part-time in the evenings from five PM to nine PM working the salad bar. That was going to work out great because I would have weekends off, and I could pick up extra time with Giant if I wanted to.

I was to report to Steak in the Sack on Monday morning, and I would be trained. I would work in the prepping area and making sandwiches. It was the weekend and I thought let me go have some fun and meet up with some friends. I found myself on the avenue playing Bid Whist, and then some one on one tonk. We played one dollar a game, one dollar for best hand, and one dollar for the high card flipped. I went home with a little more than what I came with, so that day to me was successful.

I finally called Tyrone. I told him I finally found employment, and he seemed genuinely happy for me. Tyrone told me I could get whatever I needed from him until I got paid. I told him I was good. One thing my mother always taught me was to be fully self-sufficient and never to lean on a man for nothing. She said to always be prepared to be hurt, let down, and destroyed by a man. My mother said to do for yourself because in the end the man will feel you owe him and will be ready to collect payment any way he can.

That Sunday, we went to the movies and when it was over, he took me home. He opened the door for me and waited until I got in safely before he walked off to get back in his car and go home. I ate, talked to my sister and nephew, and made my way to the showers before calling it a night. Tyrone had called, telling me he had a great time spending the afternoon with me and wanting to know when can we hook up again. I told him I would call to let him know. I was planning to spend the weekend at my stepmom's, so he would have to come there and pick me up and would have to meet her as well. He agreed.

I was on the playground playing with my niece when he pulled up and that time he was in a Denali truck. I was Black and chromed out with video in the front and back and a great sound system. I took my niece by the hand and Tyrone followed us to meet mom. My mom came out and I introduced them to each other. The last thing my mom told him was that if he hurt me, she would hurt him. Tyrone nodded then turned around and opened the door for us to exit. I told her I would be back, and Tyrone smiled at her and told her to have a good evening. Tyrone also said he would bring me in early.

I laughed because I could see that Tyrone had a way with women. He felt he could charm his way with my mother, so he felt he could have me. However, he needed to know I was good at recognizing that con shit. Game recognized game, and I learned from the best.

True to his word, he bought me back to my mom's by ten PM, and asked if I wanted to take a road trip with him the next day. I told him I would have my niece with me, and he asked me to bring her along. We decided not to go, but instead we went to the mall and he bought my niece a big balloon and got us some Snickerdoodles. He stopped and got my mom and me a pack of cigarettes, and then we called it a day. I guess he thought buying my niece a balloon and my mom a pack of cigarettes would put him in the game with me.

My mom talked to me after I got in. She told me he seemed sneaky and it was something about him that she didn't like. My mom said that she just couldn't put a finger on it. A mother's intuition was good to have because she had been around for a while, and had encountered the same shit we were to go through. She was actually speaking from experience and that was a good teacher.

Sunday rolled around, and I knew I had to be on my way home to get ready for work the next day. Tyrone called and asked what time would I be ready to leave, and I gave him a time and he was there. I kissed my mother goodbye then hugged and kissed my nieces. I gave my love to my siblings as I headed on out of the door, promising I would be over there again in the next two weeks. My oldest niece began to cry, and I assured her that I would be back. I also told my niece that she could call me whenever she wanted. I wiped her tears away, and I left out the door.

When I got outside, Tyrone was in a green Nissan Sentra. I asked him about the truck and he said he let his nephew use it, and he just grabbed the car. We stopped in Barry Farms for a few to see his cousin and that gave me time to talk to Peaches and catch up on what's been going on around the way. Tyrone would always disappear out the backdoor and his cousin would eventually follow, and I was left there to wonder where he went off to.

I grabbed my phone and called him but it went to voicemail, so I tried calling him from Peaches' phone and it did the same thing. I walked to the backdoor, hoping he would be out there but he wasn't. I told Peaches I had to be on my way home and she understood. She could tell I was upset, even though I really wasn't trying to show it. I walked to *Anacostia Station* and waited about twenty minutes before the P-Six showed up to take me home. I put my music in my ears and before I reached my stop, my phone was buzzing with a call from Tyrone. I ignored it and continued listening to my music as I walked the short distance from the stop to the house.

Once I got in, I was irritated as hell. I didn't want to talk, eat, or play around. I told my sister and nephew I was having a bad day, and then went upstairs to shower and get in bed. When I got under the water, I suddenly burst out in tears. My gut was saying he was messing around, but my head kept saying he just got caught up with some of his friends and lost track of time.

Once I put on my pajamas I listened to his voice message, begging me to forgive him. He said that his phone went dead and he had no way of contacting me until he was able to get back to his cousin's house and charge it. He said that wanted to make it up to me, but I just cut my phone off and went to sleep.

*****

It was going into December, and my birthday was right around the corner. Giant called me for another interview, and my start date would be on my birthday. The hiring manager was willing to give me my birthday off and allow me to start the following day, but I told her it was ok. I wasn't planning on doing anything, so I would be able to work.

Tyrone kept trying to reach me, and I continued to send his calls to voicemail. He would hear from me when I got good and ready to talk and right now wasn't a good time. When I left the interview at Giant, I went to work at my first job, and I basically threw myself into my work. When it was time to close, I stayed late to help the dishwashing person get caught up with her dishes and I helped the wait staff replenish their tables with sugar, salt, pepper, forks, knives, and spoons. The silverware was rolled up tight and neatly then placed them on each table.

When I arrived home, Tyrone was there and this time he was in a silver Range Rover. I asked him how many vehicles did he have, and he said he had four. The other vehicle was a Mercedes-Benz. He said it was in the shop, and he would let me take a vehicle of my choice to help me get around town. *Thanks but no thanks, I will catch the bus if I needed to go somewhere, I thought to myself.*

As luck would have it I lived only ten minutes away from both jobs, so I was good to go. Tyrone had flowers and candy in his car for me and offered them as an apology for leaving me stranded while he handled some business. I asked him what did he do for a living, and he simply told me that he gets money. I left that alone. I was always taught that some things are best left unsaid, so that you can never be called as a witness once shit hits the fan. I was not going to be anyone's codefendant on any case. I would just have to watch myself and pay attention to the warning signs.

I gave in to him and thanked him for the flowers and candy. There was a card attached and as I opened it a ring fell out. Tyrone asked me if I would be his girl/partner for life. I didn't know what to say, so I remained quiet. The envelope on the box of candy had to my love written in bold letters on it. He asked me to refrain from opening it until I was alone and in my room. I agreed to do so.

I held on to the ring then Tyrone reached out for it and placed it on my left ring finger. He asked me to be his girl/partner again, and I said ok. Tyrone kissed me like he was longing for that moment. I had not been in a relationship since I had my last set of twins in two thousand and seven and wasn't looking for anyone, but it just happened. Tyrone gave me a set of keys to his apartment and told me to feel free to come over anytime. He asked me if I would keep the Range Rover so that I could get around, and I agreed.

I took him to his apartment, gave him a kiss, dropped him off, and then I was on my way back home. My sister came in and asked about the truck that was parked in front of the house, and I told her my friend had given it to me to use for a while. She just told me to be careful, and I said that I would.

My sister knew how quick I fell for guys, and I knew she was only looking out for my best interest. If anyone didn't know better, you would think it was the oldest. She was like the mother hen who protected her little chicks, and to ensure that her baby would have nothing or no one to put her in harms way in any way, shape, form, or fashion.

My sister was a protector and she wanted to guard me from all the evil that was out there in this cruel world. She knew of the demons our father and I had and she just wanted the best from me. I didn't want to let my sister down. We had been away from each other for years and I wanted to gain her trust again.

When I was alone in my room, I opened the envelope and five crisp one hundred dollar bills were tucked neatly inside. I called Tyrone to thank him, but the call went to voicemail again. I worked the remaining of the week then went over my mom's house like I promised I would and spent some time with them.

I gassed up the truck and made a pit stop for some cookies for my niece and sister then I got me and mom a pack of cigarettes and headed towards her house. I called Tyrone once I got situated, and he promised that he would come over to see me. However, that never happened. I called his phone at around nine PM to see what was his delay, and again I never received an answer.

I jumped in the truck and headed to the Southeast to see what he was up to. I guessed that Tyrone figured he could tell me anything, and I would be alright with it and sometimes it was like that. I always went on a person's word. Your word is your bond, and you should always be able to stand firm on it and never should it waiver.

When I pulled up on Firth Sterling Avenue, and I saw Tyrone leaning against a car on the driver's side. I couldn't see who was behind the wheel, but my stomach was doing flips. I got out the truck and proceeded to walk towards him. He acknowledged me then waved his hand for me to come closer. As I approached the car, he introduced me to the guy who was driving then I stepped back. My heart had skipped a beat because my first thought was that it was a female, and that he had got caught up in his shit. The guy passed him a paper bag and then he drove off.

Tyrone turned towards me then gave me a hug and kissed me gently on the lips. After that we walked toward his cousin's house. Tyrone went on to tell me that his phone was out of commission, and that he would have to get another one. In the meantime, he said that he would be using his nephew's phone. He told me that he had some business to handle early in the morning, and asked if I could drop him off at home. I asked where was the other cars or the Denali, and he said he had to have some work done on the Mercedes-Benz, that the Denali was with his nephew, and the Sentra was acting up. I insisted that he take the truck, but he refused.

Tyrone got in the truck and we left to return to his cousin's house. He spent an hour and a half upstairs, and once again I was left downstairs all alone. Peaches was upstairs and she never knew I was downstairs, so I just made myself comfortable and played games off my phone until he was ready to go. Tyrone finally came downstairs to tell me what he needed to do was taking a little longer than expected, and that I should just go on home. I left and went to hang on the avenue for a while to play cards, and then I went back to mom's house.

Sunday morning, I got up a little early. I cooked breakfast for everyone, washed the dishes, showered, and then I was on my way back home. I never did receive a call from Tyrone, and I just let things be the way they were. When Tyrone called me late that night, I told him I had to get up early. He wanted to come get the truck, and I asked could he wait until in the morning. I wasn't going to have my sister to deactivate the alarm system just to meet him outside to get the truck. On top of that, I had taken my meds and I was truly not able to walk downstairs.

Tyrone agreed that he would come to my job and get the key. That was settled and I snugged up under my blanket and fell back to sleep. That morning was rush hour at the job. Tyrone got there about five minutes before I walked in. I gave him the key and went on about my day. We had standing room only, and I was still a little groggy from my meds. I really wasn't feeling being there that morning. My birthday was two days away and I would be starting my job at Giant today, and I was gung ho ready.

I finished the day and felt a lot better when it came to an end. It was time for me to make it next door to Giant. When I arrived, I was brought to the back where produce shared a space with the salad bar person. I was told what was expected for me to do daily and showed how to break the bar down, clean it, close down, and set it back up for the next day. I knew I could handle this job, and I was eager to get started on it.

The supervisor over the salad bar watched and hovered over me, making sure I paid attention to what was taught to me, and I think I even surprised myself. I cut the fruit up, cleaned all the bowls, wiped down the salad bar, swept and mopped my area, and then it was time to clock out. The manager told me it was going to be a pleasure working with me and I said likewise. I went home and laid back to watch TV, but then I decided to read a book on my sister's Kindle and called it a day. I showered and fell fast asleep.

When I went to work the next day it was a slow day, so that allowed me to prep a lot of things and stock up the front refrigerator for the cooks. The day was passing by slow and since we didn't receive many customers the owner was letting people go home early. I asked if I could leave and once he checked my area, I was free to go.

I went home to rest up, so I could be prepared to work at five PM. I left the house at four-thirty PM and once I got to the shopping center, I stood outside and smoked a cigarette. I would only be in there for a couple of hours to finish off my training, and then I would officially start the next day. The next day was also be my birthday!

When I arrived home, my brother-in-law had cooked and everyone wished me an early happy birthday, and I actually found myself teary eyed. Just the mere thought of finally being back home with family made me choke up. Tyrone called as we were finishing dinner and asked me to come outside. I opened the front door and there Tyrone was standing in front of the silver Range Rover. He passed me flowers, a teddy bear, and an envelope. Tyrone wished me a happy birthday. He told me that he would be away, but he wanted to drop my gifts off to me before he headed out of town.

Tyrone reached in the truck and pulled out a small German chocolate cake and gave it to me. I thanked Tyrone, and then he went on his way. I took my gifts in the house, placing the cake on the kitchen counter, I told my family they could cut it whenever they wanted to then I went upstairs. My nephew asked if I would come downstairs to play a game with him and I did. We played well into the night until he had to go to bed to prepare for school the next day, and I had to prepare for work.

I went in the room and looked at the bear Tyrone had given me. It had sad eyes like me, and I wondered did he even notice I was sad, lonely, and depressed. I opened the envelope and there was five one hundred dollar bills. I began to wonder what it was he did for a living. I knew I couldn't and wouldn't be with another drug dealer. That part of my life was gone, and I didn't ever want it to resort back to that. I wanted my life to be one of a working and able body who is able to make money the legal way while paying taxes and voting. I wanted to be a regular old Dudley Do Right.

My life suddenly took a turn for the worse. The following weekend, I decided to take Tyrone up on his offer that if and when I wanted to get away, I could always go over to his place. I did just that. I caught the bus to *Fairfax Village* and walked up the street to his apartment building then tried to enter the front door. I placed the key in the lock and as I turned it, I heard it click back. Not understanding what was going on, I did it again then I heard the same clicking sound. It was as if someone was relocking the door I was trying to unlock.

Finally, the knob twisted and low and behold there stood Tyrone, who was supposed to be out of town, looking dumbfounded. He tried to push me back from the door, and I was pushing my way inside. Tyrone said he had someone in there doing something, and I couldn't come in at the moment. I said I had to use the bathroom and when he kept denying me, I burst into the apartment then went straight towards the bathroom.

As I approached the door, I looked to my right where his bedroom was and saw a heavyset lady sitting with a crack stem, rocks, beer, and a lighter in front of her. I asked him what the fuck was going on and he said nothing. The lady looked even more shock than I did. She asked me why did I have a key to her place, and what was I doing there. I asked if this was really her place and she said yes it was hers.

I looked at Tyrone who all of a sudden got eerily quiet, and I hit him in his face. He tried to wrestle me to the floor, and I kicked and bit him then I pulled out my knife. I was ready to cut him to shit. I asked him where was the truck, and then she chimed in and said that her truck needed repairs and that it was not his truck.

What else was he lying to me about? She asked me who I was and I really couldn't find an answer, so she introduced herself as being Tyrone's wife. She told me that they were separated but nonetheless, they were married. She went on to say that he was a dealer, but he also smoked crack and that's what they were doing before I burst up in the house.

Tyrone looked defeated. He had no words to offer me. I kicked him in his nuts, threw the keys in his face, and then I walked out and slammed the door behind me for full effect. Tyrone ran down the street to where I was waiting for the bus to give me some bullshit lies. I told him to go away before I did something I would later regret and have to pay a hefty penalty for. Tyrone just wouldn't listen. I pulled my knife out and asked him to get away from me, and when he didn't I sliced his face up and walked away.

Tyrone ran behind me and grabbed my hair. He tried to pull me down, and I commenced to kick him and I swung my knife any way that I could. I sliced his arm and neck, and he also had cuts on his hands from where he tried to take the knife from me and couldn't. Tyrone called me a deranged bitch, and then I cut him some more. He got away from me and asked someone to call nine-one-one. Tyrone was bleeding profusely, and I didn't care. I hoped that he would die from the wounds, but I had no such luck.

I boarded the bus then I went to the avenue and played cards, not once thinking of the scars I left on him or the mental scars he left with me. I wanted him dead, and I was seeking to fulfill that request. I called Peaches to tell her what happened, and she said she was glad that he got caught up in his shit. I asked her if she knew about this and she said yes. Peaches said that she just didn't want to see me hurt, and she felt that he would change his ways from being with me.

I asked Peaches if she knew that he smoked crack, and she said yes. She even admitted to smoking, and I was thrown for a loop. I never saw that coming. Maybe I was just green to the facts that were right in front of me and ignored them, actually thinking I had found true love in him. I stopped going around Barry Farms for a while. I felt betrayed by all parties involved and just needed to concentrate on me. It seemed like I could only attract drug dealers or crackheads to be with. I had to do better.

CHAPTER SIX

Christmas was approaching, and I made my way to see Peaches. We talked and I listened to her speak her peace, and I said what I had to say then that was that. We remained friends but agreed that when she was getting ready to smoke, to let me know so I could leave and give her some privacy.

A few weeks had passed and I went to the rec and played a few games of pool and ping pong. There was a guy just hanging around. He spoke to me, and I spoke back. He came over and introduced himself as Gunsmoke, but said everyone called him *Big T*. That was an odd nickname. Big T said that he got the nickname from his father. That when he was younger, he would watch a lot of westerns. He would put his thumb and forefinger in a gun like fashion and pretend to shoot people and the name stuck.

We sat outside and talked for a while, and then Big T walked me to the station so I could get on the bus and head home. He gave me his phone number then I gave him my phone number. We agreed that we would take it slow because I just had got out of a nasty relationship that ended bad. He talked a lot about his children, who he had contact with and he would visit each of them whenever he could. I thought that was a wonderful thing. A man actually being there for his kids.

We began to get serious around March, which was also his birthday month. I never questioned him when he would walk off with his friends and come back sweating profusely. I just thought he was a hot natured person. I would learn differently really fast. One evening when I got off work early, I went to see him. He met me at the station and we walked to the rec center. We were sitting on the bench, and he began to vomit. I asked if he was okay and Big T said he was sick. I asked if he wanted me to go get him some crackers and a ginger ale. Big T said a ginger ale would be fine.

I walked to the store and when I returned to the bench, he was bent over retching. I went in the rec center and came out with some wet paper towels. I wiped his face and let him drink the cold soda. Big T said he was dope sick.

I asked, "Do you do dope?"

I never saw that coming. I really liked that young man and I guessed that I could look pass the dope because he straight up told me that he had a habit. He didn't lie to me about it. I reached in my wallet and pulled out a twenty dollar bill. I told him to go get his medicine, and that I would be waiting for him to come back. He finally made it back and I could see he was feeling a lot better. I made a mental note that I would go with him next time to see who he copped from just in case I decided to get one.

Big T was a snorter, and he said that he had got two for fifteen dollars and had bought some cigars with the rest. I didn't care. I had given the money to him and wasn't looking for anything in return except honesty. That would go a long way with me. I knew that he wasn't working and that he only did side jobs when needed, so I left him forty dollars to help him get through the week. He thanked me then walked me to the station. Big T waited until I was seated on the bus then he called and talked to me until I got home.

On his birthday, we went to the movies, out to eat, and then to a motel. He was staying with his niece and brothers and there was no room for him to have company there. I would never bring anyone to my sister's house to entertain because I had a nephew there and respected him as well as my sister and brother-in-law. We stayed at the motel until the next morning then left at checkout time. We walked to the mall and I waited for him to get on the bus before I turned to walk home.

It was easy to talk to Big T and not once had he done anything to hurt or harm me. We were at the rec center the following day and who came in but Tyrone. I shook my head.

He saw me and Big T together, and then yelled out, "My cousin stole my girl from me!"

Cousin? Oh shit, here we go, I thought to myself. Big T never knew I had dealings with Tyrone but since he blurted it out, I wasn't going to deny it. I told Big T what went on and he that said he had already heard about it. He then told Tyrone that he couldn't miss what he never had then we walked out.

How could these two be related? I asked myself. They were totally different. I could deal with Big T doing the dope as long as he didn't lie to me, steal from me, or cheat on me. I would be okay. For me, I was instantly in love. I went and got his nickname tattooed on my chest. I just knew we would be together forever.

Big T introduced me to all the boys he hung around with. They were cool, and yes they all got high. One of his friends said he was about to make a run for some, and he asked who wanted something. Big T put the money in my hand, and he asked if I would also stop at the store. I didn't mind. That would help me to see who I needed to see and do what I intended to do and that was to buy me a bag. I got Big T two for fifteen dollars, and I got me a twenty dollar bag. Since I was sneaking, I couldn't ask if anyone had any works so I could shoot up. Once we got back to the rec center, I excused myself and went to the bathroom. I took a couple of blows in there, and the drain came pretty fast. That was some good shit. I was feeling real good. My voice got low and sultry, and I knew at that instance that I was high.

Trying to be low key about it, I steered away from Big T. I found all types of stuff to keep me occupied. I must've nodded off because Big T was tapping me. I told him I was tired, and that I needed to leave before it got late. He walked me to the station to catch the bus. Once I boarded the bus, my phone immediately rang with Big T on the other end. We talked until I got home then well into the night. We talked about our likes and dislikes, family, what we wanted out of life, and so on until it was time for me to get some sleep. The dope still had an effect on me, and I drifted off to sleep.

I woke up the next morning and found myself reaching for that little packet that made me feel good. I wanted to be right before I met up with Big T. I did my routine of showering and primping before the mirror to make sure I was looking alright. I noticed how glossy my eyes looked. My sister didn't know about drugs and the effects it has on people so I knew I could get away with just saying it was my meds working.

I went to the rec center and as I approached the door, I saw Big T hanging with a few guys in the corner. He waved me over and introduced me to his friends as his lady. I was brimming with joy after being called his lady. Never had I ever heard those words come out of a man's mouth. He gave me time, attention, and respect. Whenever I came around, his concern and focus was on me.

I sat and talked to him. I told him I was looking for a place and would like for him to come with me. He agreed and we made plans. I left that evening, feeling as if I was on cloud nine. I had been thinking about having Big T come live with me. I didn't like the living arrangements he had. He was going from one family member's house to the next, and having to sleep upright on the couch. No one should have to live like that.

My brother had invited us to stay with him and his girlfriend. She had two kids and still allowed us to have their bedroom. We discussed payments and came up with an arrangement. I would still go back and forth between her place and my sister's. My brother had a Mercedes-Benz that he was willing to let me purchase, and all I had to do was get the rotor for the tire or something or another. I don't know too much about cars, but whatever the thingamajig was it cost me fifty dollar. I had my uncle put it on and the Mercedes-Benz was ready to hit the road. My brother had also purchased another vehicle from a car place on Good Hope Road and we traded vehicles often.

I searched the paper and found a man who was renting his basement. It had an entrance off the kitchen and I could enter from the outside and just make sure the door to the kitchen remained locked so no one could enter. The place had a bathroom in there and a place where I could put a hot plate, so I didn't have to go upstairs to use the kitchen. All systems said go. I moved my stuff from my sister's house and Big T was there to help me. It felt like a weight had been lifted off my shoulders. I could do what I wanted, whenever I wanted and not have to walk on eggshells. I wanted freedom from everyone and everything. I just wanted to do me.

I went to *William's Warehouse* and purchased a refrigerator and a hot plate then we headed to the grocery store. I had an air mattress and it slept pretty well for the both of us. I also purchased a TV, so that I could keep myself entertained while being there. I would usually just listen to music or read, but having a TV cut back on a lot of noise that they made upstairs. This was definitely going to take some use getting to.

Having that car and being able to get back and forth to work from Capital Heights, Maryland to Marlow Heights made things a little better. Instead of having to leave out early, I could leave fifteen minutes before I was due to be there and arrive on time. After a couple of months had passed my brother saw that we were no longer going to be there with him and his girl, he started throwing shade in the game. It was my payday and I was due to pay him some money for the car, and he started telling me the real owner of the car was looking for a payment from him. I asked him for the man's name and phone number so I could reach out to him and pay him. I figured that since it was his friend's car, we shouldn't have to do third parties and I could deal with the main source. My brother saw differently.

My brother called me at work to harass me. He said that he was coming to get the car and to make sure the title is in the glove compartment along with all this other shit. I reminded him that the tags were in my name and they were coming off, so he needed to be careful going wherever he was going. My brother didn't have a license and had always been fascinated with vehicles to please a woman. He always acted like he was the *big man* everywhere he went. I told him to come get the car, but that he would have to pick it up from where I lived. I wasn't going to be stranded at work, waiting for a bus. I had gassed the car up, so I made sure I ran the majority of the gas out before my brother thought he was going to get too far away.

By the time he came to pick up the vehicle, I left the house and sat across the street watching him as he knocked on the door and received an envelope, which contained the title. He was asking the person who answered the door about where were the tags and they explained that the tags were taken off because I had to turn them in. My brother was wondering how he was going to get home with no tags.

I yelled out, "The same way you got me on this vehicle is the same way someone is going to get you!"

He looked around, trying to see where I was. I walked out from the darkness, and he pleaded with me to give him the tags, and I said no then walked in the house. I was done. I didn't want him to call me, and I didn't want him to ask me for shit. I always told people they would need me before I needed them, and I made good on that theory because I never called him again.

That night, Big T didn't come in. Not that he was obligated, but I felt he was. I called Big T's phone and it went straight to voicemail. I knew that he didn't have it charged up, but I was also worrying about where he was and what he was doing. Sunday morning arrived and there was a knock on my door. It was Big T and he was high. I believe I was mad because I also wanted to be high, but he couldn't know about it.

Big T had a duffel bag with him, so I knew he was staying the night. I cooked breakfast and as we ate we watched some movies on the DVD. He nodded off to sleep and I snuggled next to him. It was after lunch when we both woke up, and I said I wanted to go around the way. We caught the train at Capital Heights Station and headed to Anacostia. My stomach was growling and it wasn't from being hungry. I needed to feed the hunger it had for some dope.

When we got to the station, I told him I would catch up to him. I told him that I was going to stop over a friend's house, and he said okay. I walked down to Pomeroy Road where I knew the dope boys were. I got a half of a gram and bought some works. I was going to finally be able to get high the way I've always done it by mainlining or as most people say *strike red*.

I went directly to the bathroom and cooked up the dope. I shot it up then had to sit down for a minute or two. It had my head reeling fast. The dope was excellent and when I walked out the bathroom, you would've thought I was a different person. I was so full of life. Everything seemed funny, and I began to feel the full effects and began vomiting. Big T asked if I was okay and I said it must've been what I had eaten to make me feel like that and to top it off I didn't take the medicine that was prescribed to me that day.

I was off balance and needed help just to stand up for a period of time. My stomach began to have pains and when I went to the bathroom I realized I had caught a habit. Damn! I told Big T I was ready to go and we left. When I got home, I showered and fell fast asleep. I woke up the next morning, and I was sick as a dog. I needed a fix. I grabbed my purse, not to disturb Big T, and hurried into the bathroom to cook up my dope. I got the dope in my system then grabbed my purse and walked towards the bed. Big T was just getting up, and he went into the bathroom. When he came out, he was not pleased at all. He asked when did I start shooting dope again, and I said that I wasn't. He opened his hands and there was the spoon with cotton on it and the syringe. I was caught. Lie number one.

I ran outside to get away from him, but he followed right behind me. He didn't argue or fuss. Big T said that he understood. He actually felt responsible for me getting high, and I told him he couldn't blame himself. That was me acting on my own free will. I told him I was sorry that I lied to him and that I would stop. I just couldn't, not at that time. I was too far in to stop.

The guy I was renting from began to act an ass upstairs with his company, and I asked him if he could tone the stomping and yelling down. He was drunk and told me that if I didn't like it, I could move. That was enough said. I began to look at other options quickly. We were there for two months when the basement flooded. There was a heavy rain and it caused the leaves to get into the drain, stop it up, then flood the inside. My electrical appliances started sparking, and I had to find a way to pull them from the socket. The air mattress was damaged, and I knew that it was time to go.

The guy who owned the place had made a trip out of town, and I called to tell him what happened. I sent pictures, asking to be compensated for the damages. He wasn't hearing any of that. I told him that he wouldn't be receiving any rent from me either. He threatened to take me to court. I remained there for two more months, rent free with the basement a complete disaster.

I had made contact with a lady who had an apartment available immediately. I met with her to discuss a move in date and other arrangements. I just wanted to get from out of that man's basement and fast. It started smelling of mildew. A lot of our clothes were damaged and since he refused to pay for damages, I left the place trashed. I went to pick up the U-Haul, while Big T waited on the premise, making sure the owner didn't come to do anymore damage like throwing our stuff outside. We packed the U-Haul and headed on out to our new place of residence. We moved onto Martin Luther King Junior Avenue Southeast in the Nalbert Apartment building. I was back in a familiar area. That was my old stomping grounds. I knew a lot of people in the area, and I knew a lot of drug boys. I wouldn't have to travel far now.

We unpacked and got settled in. I fixed us something to eat, and then we headed to the park so I could play a game or two of bid whist. I drank with the fellas and smoked my cigarettes then when it was all over I had some dope to go home with for both me and Big T. Big T didn't like the fact that I was a shooter. I explained to him that I didn't like the drain the dope gave me and I could get higher faster by injecting. He asked me to do him. I said no and gave him the same spill that was given to me. I told him you can't play around with the needle. I told him you'll be hooked before you know it and it happened. We both were hooked on the syringe, and one of us felt the other was getting more than they were supposed to have.

I had to tell Big T that first of all, I was the one spending the money and while we were on that subject, I told him that he needed to find a steady job to help with the bills. We wouldn't just have rent, we would also have a cable bill, an electric bill, and a phone bill. He had a government phone, so he was okay. I eventually stopped working at Steak In A Sack due to a fire then I got a job at Burger King, which was also in Marlow Heights. They wanted to give me more hours and since I got paid more there, I decided I was going to leave Giant all together. I talked to my department supervisor and told her I would remain there until they trained someone else and she agreed.

After a month had passed and I saw they weren't looking to hire anyone, I told her I would be leaving for good by the end of the week. She seemed a bit disappointed in knowing I was leaving. I went home and spoke to Big T about him finding employment again, and Big T said that he was looking. I already knew that was lie because his main focus was being in Barry Farms at their rec center with his friends and getting a free high.

Once I got my feet planted in Burger King, I asked the manager about hiring my boyfriend as a stocker/maintenance man, and she agreed. The next day, Big T and I arrived and the manager had him fill out an application then hired him on the spot. He would work the same days as me, but also on some weekends when the big truck came for deliveries. I told Big T that the first check he receives would be for him to do as he wanted to, but after that we'll be dividing things in half except my phone bill which was my responsibility.

Payday rolled around and when we left work, we walked across the mall to the liquor store to cash our checks. Big T said he was going to give me some money. I was impressed. I got a bottle of Patron then we went home. True to his word, he gave me some money. It was twenty dollars.

I looked at that money then looked at him, and asked, "Are you sure you're able to part with this much?"

He said I could use it to buy *us* a bag of dope. I laughed at that thought then walked out the door. He received a check for over five hundred dollars and gave me twenty dollars. I just shook my head and kept walking towards the park to see who was up there that I could cop from. I bought a gram then bought some syringes and played a few games of cards. I decided to go over a friend's house and get high. I didn't want to be around Big T because I was heated, and just didn't want to deal with him at all.

I sat in my friend's house and she allowed me to go do my stuff in her bedroom, while she and her male friend were in the front smoking crack. When I was done, I took a seat with them and listened to the crackling sound of the fire touching the rock and saw it melt down. I watched the cloud form, and then I watched as she sucked the smoke from the glass bowl. Oh how I longed to try that.

I asked her for a hit. She gave me her glass bowl and a rock then I fired it up. Damn, I hadn't felt like that in a long time. I reached in my pocket and pulled out fifty dollars then I asked her to call someone. She did and right before they arrived, we walked to the store where I could purchase my own glass stem and the stuff I needed to get me started.

When we arrived back to her house, I was antsy. I was waiting to hit my own rock and feel the euphoria I'd been waiting for. When her guy arrived I gave him the fifty dollars for some more and when he left, we smoked well into the night. Big T continued to ring my phone, and I continued to send the calls to voicemail. I got in the house after three AM, feeling lovely. I lit a cigarette, drank my liquor, and shot some more dope. Remembering the twenty dollars that Big T had given me, I gave him that much dope.

I decided to sleep in the front room, so that I could enjoy my high. No sooner than I got a good nod in, Big T came out the room and asked me if I could hit him. I really would have liked to hit him, but in a different manner. I wanted to clock him right upside his head. I didn't get much rest and before I knew it, it was time to go to work. I was in training to become a manager and had to learn all areas of the fast food restaurant. I was on the grill and making sandwiches then still had to man the cash registers and send people on breaks.

I was a quick learner, so I knew I wouldn't have a problem with learning all I needed to grasp onto. The manager took me in the office and showed me how to do a food order sheet. We had to go in the freezer and count what was there and that was how we determined what was needed for the next week. There was a time when we miscalculated the fry count and had to borrow from another store as well as the buns.

I was constantly watching the clock, anticipating for the time to leave so I could go home, get high, and chill. I got so high that night, celebrating my moving up the ladder that I had to call in the next day. I said I was getting sick from being in that freezer with no jacket. They said okay, and I continued to get high all day. I really didn't like to keep money on me, so I made a decision that I would go open a bank account and receive direct deposit. I went into *SunTrust Bank* at around two PM that afternoon, and deposited some money to open a checking account, leaving enough money out so that I could get high when I left the bank.

I immediately called my friend and asked her to call her guy then I was on my way to her house. Big T wanted to tag along, and I let him. I asked him how much money did he have and he said none. I couldn't believe he had spent all his money. When I asked him where and what did he spend it on Big T said he loaned a couple of friends some money and was helping his daughter out. I was totally pissed and it showed. *How could he help all these people out and not look out for your household?* I asked myself.

Big T threw back in my face that I told him that he could do whatever he wanted to with his first check. Yes, I did say that but I also thought he would be a little responsible and ask if he could help out with anything. I guess my thinking was what got me into the predicaments I seemed to get into. Being the one to always save everybody, I gave him some money so that he could get what he wanted and I could do my thing.

When Big T saw us smoking crack, he couldn't believe it. Big T asked if he could try it and I asked him why would he want to do that.

He said that he wanted to do everything I did.

I found no logic in that. It just showed me that I would be the one who supplies, and he would reap from the benefits. It seemed as if he had done this before, but he claimed that he never did. He smoked hard and longer than we did. Big T seemed to be dropping rocks in the stem faster and faster. I had to put some brakes on him. *How was he going to sit up in there and smoke more than me, and he didn't put up one dame dime?* I asked myself. Nope, that wasn't going to happen.

After two or three days of being M.I.A. at work, I decided to finally show up. I had told the manager that I was real sick and still wasn't feeling too good. She was really lenient with me. She even mentioned to me that she was glad I got Big T in there to work. Big T took a load off of a lot of people. The days I was off, Big T showed up to work and it showed in his paycheck. We paid the rent and electric, and still had enough money to blow on getting high.

I went to the liquor store and purchased a bottle of Velicoff since it was cheap, and I could have more money for my product. Getting high everyday had begun to take a toll on me, and I was beginning to get tired of leaving my home in the Southeast and go to work in Marlow Heights. I tried to get a transfer to the Burger King in Eastover, but since they were privately owned I was unable to transfer. I would have to leave Marlow Heights and place an application in with them.

I decided to stay a little while longer and as luck has it, the manager who was training me to be a manager was transferred to another location. We had a new manager come in and everything changed. He never asked anyone about how their schedule was working for them. He just up and changed the schedule without notifying us that he was doing so. He just yelled out that schedules had been changed. He said to check your name, dates, and times before you leave. The manager told us that if we had any questions he would be able to meet with us upon submitting a written request.

That was some bullshit! *How was he just going to come in and uproot us from our normal schedules to fit his need?* I asked myself. I didn't know how he did it, but it was done. I was now on the evening shift from four PM until twelve AM. I had a problem with that. I rode transit and it was difficult getting a P-Six at twelve-forty-five AM because that was the time I would be at the bus stop after cleaning up the store. There was no way in hell I would be able to keep that shift.

The new manager, John, told me if I was going for manager I had to be able to work all shifts. I nipped that in the bud real quick by telling him I no longer wanted the manager-in-training position. I would rather keep my early shift and just be an ambassador of Burger King. It was granted, and I stayed on the eight AM until four PM shift and I was still able to keep my pay. He even asked me if I could do every other weekend, and he would give me a two dollar raise and I agreed. Now I was receiving a pay of seventeen-twenty-five an hour and I was the ambassador.

My job description was to meet and greet the customers, pass out samples of new items, and take votes on their likes and dislikes. I also worked closely with management to help with breaks and count the safe at the beginning of my shift and when changing over for the next shift. Having that position allowed me to maneuver around, and I was able to take money from drawers by over ringing items or cancelling them out. Each day I went home with nothing less than two hundred dollars. I was able to get high each day. That was going to become a great come up for me.

Another manager was training this young lady for the drive thru register. The thing about it was that she was slow and not able to keep her money in tack, meaning she couldn't count. I helped her lose her job because it was me who had emptied her drawer and took out a stack of twenty dollar bills that she was unable to count for. She was unable to explain what happened, and by the end of the week she was fired. I moved around the store freely and since I wasn't the only one going in registers, I could never be blamed.

Management had a meeting and since I sat in on every meeting, I was able to stay at least two to three steps ahead of them. I knew who they were looking at to fire and who they thought was stealing. If anyone crossed my path, I set it up so good that they would be fired by the end of the week if not the same day. Working there became easy money and it allowed me to gain the trust of my coworkers as well as upper management.

I had to train two people and it went well. They were quick learners and easy to adapt to the atmosphere. The young lady had come to me at the end of her shift and asked how could she get her schedule changed because she had a daughter in daycare and would have to pick her up at a certain time or it would cost her extra. I spoke to John and pleaded her case. John wanted to get rid of her but he knew she was an asset to the company, so he obliged and asked her what hours she would be able to work.

Everything worked out and the Burger King of Marlow Heights had risen to the top of the billboard. We were now the number one fast food restaurant in that area of Maryland. I left that evening feeling drained. I needed a quick *pick me up*, and then I would be okay. I called a friend of mine who agreed to pick me and Big T up, and all I needed to do was buy him a bag of dope. It was all settled.

I had called my friend to meet me at the house, and I told him what I needed. He delivered everything in a timely manner and before I was able to shower and change into something more comfortable, I had to get a bag in my system. When I ran the water, I noticed that Big T had snuck outside. He was talking to the dope boy and asking for credit. I didn't want any parts of that. I never wanted to start a credit line with the dope boy. If something was to happen there was no telling what he would do to get his money.

I jumped in the shower, and when I came out I noticed my purse was opened wide. I looked in it and saw that my wallet had been opened. It was noticeable because it had two snaps on it and they were undone. I knew how much money I had, but as I searched the folds of my wallet fifty dollars was missing. *Now he's stealing from me? Why?* I questioned to myself. All he had to do was ask, but that seemed too much like right.

Big T still hadn't come inside, so I slipped on some sweat pants and a top then went downstairs. He was in the front talking to someone that he apparently knew, and I stood in the doorway of the building waiting to confront him. As his friend turned away to leave, Big T came in the building. Judging by the look on his face, he had to know what my look was saying.

Before I could get the words out, Big T said, "Baby, Blackman gave us a deal and I got fifty dollars out your wallet to put with what I had."

"Exactly what do you have?" I asked.

He pulled out a wad of twenty dollar bills, and I couldn't believe my eyes. Big T told me that   we would talk about this upstairs then we ran upstairs to our apartment. He told me how John had left three registers unattended and no one was in the area, so he swiped some cash from each one. I was flabbergasted. I never thought Big T would have the gall to pull that kind of stunt in the work place, but he did. He had just about as much guts as I had, yet and still he never knew what I did. I went by the old saying that what you don't know won't hurt you, and if I tell you I'm going to have to kill you.

We went in the bedroom and sat down on the bed. He handed me an envelope. I looked inside and there was well over nine hundred dollars. He said that was for rent. Big T then told me that he was going to show me what he had got for two hundred and fifty dollars. He pulled out so much crack and dope that I thought I was going to faint. He had three eight balls, which weighed three point five grams, and two spoons of dope.

The guy Big T was talking to asked if he thought that we, as a team, could move a sleeve of heroin. That was a lot of dope. The actual weight was two hundred and thirty-four grams. I said that I didn't have the clientele for dope, but I could ask around in the park to see who's who and what they're selling. We would have to find out the quality of their dope as well as what we were going to put out.

The guy had told Big T that he would give him one hundred testers to see what the people thought of it. If we decide to get it, we would bag it ourselves and cut it if it had to be cut. My mind kept telling me yeah go ahead and do it, but my gut was saying it's the wrong thing to do. I told Big T that I would think about it, but right now all I wanted to do was drink, smoke, and shoot some dope.

We had a ball in the quietness of our bedroom. We pumped the CD player and turned the phones off, not wanting to be disturbed. We heard a loud knock on the door, and since you need a key to get through the front door it definitely had to be someone in the building. I turned the music down a little and yelled out who is it? It was the landlord. I asked her to give me a minute, and then I would knock on her door. The good thing about the building we occupied was that the landlord was in the building. The bad thing about it was she and her nosey ass husband watched who came and went and how many times they did. It was like being under the microscope of neighborhood watchers.

I got the envelope that I received from Big T and grabbed the four hundred dollars from my wallet then headed across the hall to pay her the money. Whenever we gave her cash, it seemed like she would always try to rush us out her house. When the cash hits her hand, she was licking her lips and her eyes got bugged out. I laughed because if she actually knew my thoughts we would probably be fighting.

Our landlords were creatures of habit. On Mondays, Wednesdays, and Fridays, Pea Pod from Giant would deliver their groceries. On Tuesdays and Fridays a laundry person would pick up early then drop their clothes back by one PM. On weekends they were gone. I had come up with a master plan to rob the household. I had to plan this carefully. It's amazing how the brain works when getting stoned out your mind.

Big T and I had finally dozed off to sleep when the alarm rang for us to get up to prepare for work. I really wanted to call in, but I knew it would raise suspicion. Reluctantly, I got up and showered then put on my uniform. Big T followed suit. When we arrived at work it was the same old shit with John wanting to change the schedules. I wasn't having it. I was on the morning shift and that's where I preferred to stay.

Upper management had come up with a plan of their own. They felt I would be better on the evening shift where I could maneuver around and get the sales back to where they needed to be. Being an ambassador was a lot of work, and I had to be open for suggestions from both customers and management. I was in the process of making samples and an uproar came from the back of the restaurant. It was a delivery guy making a fuss over the stock we ordered. He forgot to load the fries and we had to go borrow from another store again. This was going to be one hell of a day.

By lunch time, I was sitting in the office looking at the schedule that had been made by John and it had me on the evening shift. I would start out with the two PM to ten PM shift then go to the four PM to twelve AM shift. They also offered me a pay raise, and I was to stop being the ambassador and begin training as an evening manager. I would have to come in at noon for training and get off at eight PM for the next three weeks. I was already a step ahead because I had learned how to make all the sandwiches, how to flame broil, do inventory, order food, and count the registers and the safe.

The upper management team wanted to see me in action, so I showed them what I could do. They were truly impressed by the way I moved in the kitchen. I only needed to be shown once, and then I could do it. I learned very well from being in North Carolina working in a cafeteria. I received my manager's uniform and there was a lot of people that were mad but I didn't care. My mind was focused on getting the job done by any means necessary.

Within two weeks, I had fired three people and hired four. One young man was on top of his game. He came to work every day, greeted everyone, and did what he was supposed to do. I offered him the job as the ambassador and he accepted. I knew that the evening team was going to be a great.

As the months passed the evening crew had best attendance, best grill person, more sales, and cashier of the month. We were taking Burger King to another level! My pockets were even getting fatter and no one expected a thing. That evening, I counted the safe, counted down the registers, and then headed out the door to catch the bus. Big T came out a few minutes later, and he had a pocket full of money. I knew we were going to meet our boy before we headed in, and I could hardly wait.

As we got closer to home, we called our guy and he met us. I went on the avenue to find someone who had some works and to buy a new glass stem for us both. We got in the house, took our clothes off, showered, and then got high all night long. Neither of us had to work the next day, so we made sure that we had enough money and product to last us.

The good thing was that when my schedule changed, so did Big T's. The only difference was on the weekend. I had to work every other weekend, and Big T came in only if we needed the manpower. Big T was doing a fantastic job at keeping the freezers and refrigerators cleaned, stocked, and updated by using the first in, first out method. He dated stuff and rotated frequently.

I dozed off, and when I opened my eyes again the sun was coming up. That was one hell of a nod. I took a razor blade and cut of a piece of the rock off. I put it in my stem and melted it down. It melted so fast that I knew this shit was some butter. I hit it long and deep. Bells began to ring, and I got paranoid. I heard all kinds of shit. I thought someone was on the roof trying to get in the window, so I closed it but Big T kept opening it. I got mad and told him to leave the damn thing shut. Big T told me to take a shot of dope, get a drink, and cool off. I felt he was plotting with the imaginary people on the roof that were trying to get in through the window. I thought Big T wanted me to leave the room, so he could let them in to get me.

I sat there on the bed looking at the window stupidly. I was watching and waiting but nothing ever came through the window, so I cooked up some dope and felt a lot better. I felt more calmed and relaxed. At around ten AM a knock came at the door. I already knew who it was and what she wanted. I looked in the drawer and pulled out an envelope that held the rent money then walked to the door and gave it to her. She asked me to come get the receipt, but I asked her to slide it under my door.

Big T and I got dressed and walked to the park. I wanted to play some cards, and he wanted to just get out. We stayed up there until well after ten PM then we headed on home. Big T had been up there discussing stuff over with his friend about selling dope, and I really didn't want any parts of it.

Two weeks passed, and then Big T got his wish. His guy, true to his word, gave him one hundred testers to put out but we kept the majority of them. We kept maybe ninety for ourselves.

Big T told his guy it was a go then he came pass and dropped the package off over to the house. Big T knew nothing about cutting the dope, so I had to do it. I had learned how to do that while being with an ex-boyfriend. He showed me everything there was to know about cooking dope, crack, selling, bagging, and storing it in a safe place.

I was taught to never lay your head where your drugs are, but since we lived in an apartment building where a guest had to ring the doorbell we were safe. No one would actually know we kept drugs in the apartment. We planned to make as much money as we could and keep going to work and do what we had to do. The rent and other bills were paid on time, and we had no worries.

Big T came then went and we went to our jobs as we were scheduled to do so, and then abruptly things at Burger King came to an end for me. I had picked up a dope habit and it made it harder and harder for me to go back and forth to work. When I was able to go, I had to keep dope with me so that I wouldn't become sick throughout the day. I would have to take two to three breaks just to shoot some dope in the bathroom.

One day I was in there cleaning my works and another employee walked in and saw the syringe. I tried to tell her that I was a diabetic, but she knew otherwise. She suggested that I get some help and get it fast. I couldn't go into a rehab. *What would the people there say and think of me?* I thought to myself. She had confided in me that she was an ex-heroin user and how she kicked the habit by going into a drug treatment facility. I told her that I had went to a program before and wasn't looking to go into another one. I said that I just needed to have three days off to kick this habit then I would be as good as new.

I told management that I had a death in my family and needed some time off, which I was granted. I fought long and hard to kick that dope habit. A few of my friends came to assist me, while Big T went to work. When he came home at night, I would have already showered and be in bed. The first couple of days were the worse. My bowels were loose and my stomach was empty. Whenever I tried to eat, I would vomit. They fed me bananas, and I drank juices to keep myself hydrated. I drank at least two to three bottles of water a day.

My face wasn't looking ashy anymore. I was slowly coming around. Big T was still getting high, however he stopped doing it around me. Once I was back on my feet, I still wanted to smoke crack and felt if I did some dope that I would just do it every other day. That was the bright idea I came up with.

The following week I went back to work and received cards, flowers, and money from my coworkers. It was such a lovely gesture. I had to keep the façade going. I cried a little, laughed a little, cried some more, and laughed some more. My emotions were all over the place.

When I left that evening, I looked in the envelope and saw that I had over three hundred dollars in cash and a check for five hundred dollars. That was going to be spent on some crack and some dope. Now I knew the right way to get high. I didn't get high every day, and I didn't do it a lot. That went on for a few months then I realized I could no longer do the job. I quit and looked for something closer to home. I looked for something in walking distance or in Eastover where I would only have to catch one bus to and from work.

Big T remained on the job for a few more months then he also left. He made more money selling dope than he did working at Burger King. I told him it was his decision, and as long as he paid the rent or a portion of it that we would be fine. The rent was due in a couple of weeks, and I pulled all my money from the bank and Big T used what he had and it still wasn't enough. I pleaded and bargained with the landlord and made promises of having the rest of the money in a couple of weeks. I told her that Big T and I were laid off with a few others due to the labor being high. She said she would work with us because she had never had a problem with us as tenants.

The drugs were selling pretty swiftly, but just not as fast as we wished they were. I found myself stressed out and getting higher than ever and doing more and more. The money never rolled in for the rent, and the guy was on hold to receive his portion of the money. I knew right then and there that we were getting ready to lose our place. The landlady took us to court, and we met with an attorney. We made more promises and within two weeks, we had the money we needed for her and Big T's guy.

I sat Big T down and told him that we needed to end that drug game. All we were doing was robbing Peter to pay Paul, and we would soon run out of excuses. Once the package was gone and everyone received their money, we went back to working the streets. I sold dummy bags of coke, and Big T had sold dummy bags of dope. When people came to me saying the coke wouldn't melt down, I told them that it melted for me. I said maybe someone switched on you and they would purchase more.

Within two months, the landlady was turning the building over to someone else, but she gave the tenants an option to pull together and buy the building. No one was interested and by the time the new owners took over, we had enough to pay for that month. It was just a matter of time before we would be on the street. I was just counting the days because they were numbered.

I set out with a master plan. I was going to rob one of the biggest dope boys in the area. He sold dope, crack, and bottles of water for dippers. I knew his stash spots, and he would never believe I was capable of doing that to him. I walked up on the avenue and saw him sitting by himself smoking a cigarette. I went over and we made small talk. A buyer came to him and I watched his moves and where he went. He was on his way back, and I slightly turned my face in the opposite direction. He asked me if I was going to be there for a minute and I said yeah. I told him that I was waiting on my turn for the card table. He said he would be right back. He told that he was going into the gas station, and he asked if I wanted anything. For good measures, I pulled out a five dollar bill and asked him to get me some Martin's Red Hot Chips, which were undoubtedly my favorite.

As he walked to the gas station, I made my move. I got the package of coke and dope and stuffed it in my underwear then went to the card table. He came out and saw I was no longer at the table he was at, but I was now at the card table. He walked over and gave me my change. He stood there for what seemed like an eternity then someone came and whispered something in his ear. He rolled out with them, and headed to his stash spot.

As luck would have it there were a lot of people in the alley getting high and shooting dice, so when he went to get his packages they were gone. He came to the table and asked if I saw anyone go over there, and I said not while I was at the other table. He stormed back into the alley, and before you knew it shots were ringing out and people were scrambling for their lives. After busting off a few rounds, he left and vowed to find out who stole his stuff.

Once the card game was over and everything had settled down, I walked home with a feeling of satisfaction. I knew I couldn't just go out and sell it because I would be a suspect, but then again he knew that Big T and I were selling drugs. I just changed the color of the bags and resealed them. With over three thousand dollar's worth of drugs, we would be set for a minute. We got high, called some friends over, made sales, and just chilled.

Over the next few days, we made our rent money and electric bill money, but it was never paid. We used the money to get more drugs and alcohol, and didn't think twice about the rent being paid. After neglecting the rent for over two months, we were threatened by another court paper. We didn't go to court, which left only one option and was eviction. I knew I couldn't have my stuff on the streets, so I began to sell the bedroom set, TV, and other gadgets in the house to eliminate me having to carry them around. I figured we could use the money for more drugs.

I had a couple of friends who would still call and ask if they could come over. I informed them that we were in the process of moving, and we only had a bed and two folding chairs. They didn't mind at all. We entertained them for hours and by the end of the night, we had made around six hundred dollars to keep us afloat.

Every day, we were on egg shells, looking out the window to see if the eviction truck was outside. One morning, we got the shock of our lives. The truck was out there, but the landlord said it's not for us. We got lucky that day. I began to ask different people I hung out and got high with if we could leave our clothes over their place and come through and change. A couple of people agreed and soon, we had clothes all over the Southeast area. I could barely keep up with where my belongings were anymore. I just made do with what I had where I was. We would still go up to the apartment to get high and bring people over to get high and chill.

Two weeks had passed, and as I was leaving out the front door I saw the eviction people. I ran upstairs, grabbed my stem and works, threw them in a bag, and then went back out the front door. They were hitting our apartment, but there was nothing to bring out. The joke was on you landlord!

I walked pass and greeted them then I went on my way to the park. No one knew we were living from pillar to post, and I sure as hell wasn't going to broadcast it. We told people we were waiting to move into our place, but that it wasn't ready yet. It would be yet another month until the inspectors were able to come out.

We managed to be able to stay at a friend's house. After a couple of days she started acting funny, so we left and promised to come get our clothes in a few days. One of the girls by the park that I called my sister invited us to stay with her and her husband along with their daughter and granddaughter. She had recently lost her mother and was there for us when we needed her the most.

With no money and a habit from hell, I set out to do whatever I could to get me some dope. I would send Big T outside to see if he could score us some dope because I needed a fix before I could get moving. The one that I called my sister would give me money to go get some dope and she would tell me that I better not give any to Big T.

Everyone knew that if I had one ten dollar bag, Big T would get half. That was all the time, but I noticed that he wouldn't play fair with me. He would go missing and come back high as hell then swear by God and all His disciples that he hadn't had a thing. I knew a lot of dopeboys, but I wasn't trying to lay with them to get drugs. I saw the way they treated us crackheads and dopefiends when we had no money, and our next resort was to trick for it. I said I would never stand on a corner and sell my ass and meant it.

I would see older guys and they would ask me what I was getting into and if I wanted to go with them and get high. They knew I had a guy, but that never bothered them, and for that moment it didn't bother me either. I gave them sex and they gave me drugs and money as well as took me out to eat.

I made sure to save the drugs so that Big T could reap my rewards, and I wouldn't have to explain what I did to get the drugs or the money. As long as he had a box of Black and Mild's and some drugs, he was good to go. The men I went out with had other friends who didn't like to be seen on the street or driving around looking for a date, so I offered my number to them as well. That was the start of something new.

Since leaving Burger King, I had made dating a full-time job. Most men felt that since the hookers had left 14th and U Street Northwest that they could pay ten to twenty dollars for sex. In some areas you could, but just not with me. At least not in the beginning. I was getting paid two hundred to two hundred and fifty dollars per customer, and that enabled me to afford the dope and coke I needed to get me through the day and night the next part of the morning. That is if I didn't go overboard that night.

I would make sure I paid my sister/friend upfront for allowing us to stay there, then I would call the dope boy for my medicine. That went on for about three months, and then that had become a headache for me. I just didn't want to date anymore. Most men were looking for me to do things I wasn't willing to do like give up oral sex without a condom or they wanted to go in the backdoor, and that was definitely a no go. Ever since I got raped, there was a lot of things I wasn't comfortable with doing.

One day a guy called me up and said he had two friends with him, and that they were willing to spend a grand a piece on me if I allowed them to run a train on me. The money sounded good, but I had other plans. I agreed I would meet them and asked for them to text me the address and the time. I phoned a friend and asked for his gun then told him I needed his assistance. I knew I couldn't ask Big T because he was such a coward, but he would always be the first at the round table to get high. All that shit was about to come to an end and fast.

I met my friend, gave him the address, and we agreed that I would leave the door unlocked. I arrived at the designated time and the guy I was talking to, who arranged this rendezvous, let me in. He escorted me to the room to where the other two guys were sitting in the man cave and nursing some drinks. They offered me a drink and I allowed him to pour me some Patron in a glass, and I sipped on it while we got acquainted. I asked if there was some ice and he told me to make myself at home then directed me to the kitchen. While in there, I unlocked the door and called my friend then told him to make his way to the place.

When I returned to the room, we made small talk then each of us made our way to the bedroom. As I began to undress, so did the others. I crawled on the bed in a cat like fashion, purring my way to the top. I pulled the covers back and motioned with my finger for them to come join me. With a quick response, the first guy came out his tighty-whities and the other fell into pursuit, while the third guy finished nursing his drink. They asked if I wanted to take a hit before we got into it, and I said that would be nice.

As the first guy reached over to his case, which was holding all types of paraphernalia in it, a loud crashing noise came from the other side of the door. I jump up off the bed, reached for my purse which held a 9 mm in it then I pointed it at them while my friend burst through the door with his Glock pointed at them. He asked them to back themselves up to the wall and be quiet or he would shoot them.

The first guy looked at me, and said, "I really can't believe you set us up like this."

I replied, "I can't believe it either. Now when I go to the ATM these cards better be active. If not, I know where you live and we will come there. Understand?"

They each were looking pitiful as I went through their pants, shirts, jackets, and worked my way to the briefcases. Jackpot! It was a lot of money and drugs in there, and I knew I had hit the motherlode. My friend had begun to tie each of them up. He made a call and two more guys came up and helped. They were also ducked taped just for good measures. We had the other two guys to go check the ATM to make sure that they gave us the right pin numbers.

While waiting around, my friend and I decided to see what our night brought us. Calculating the money, it was close to five thousand dollars and the drugs were about a half a key of coke and two sleeves of heroin. He and I broke it down to two thousand dollars apiece then we gave the other two guys five hundred dollars each and broke down the drugs with them.

Everything checked out at the ATM, and we were free to leave. The ATM cards were good to use for two days with a limit of one thousand dollars at the machine and of course we went shopping. One of my friend's people tried to use the card again, being greedy, and was arrested. He told the police he found the card and some papers on the bus. The men could never identify him, so he was released. I knew that if they caught up to me, I was going to die or be brutally punished.

As luck would have it, I never saw them again during my addiction. I gave my sister/friend three hundred dollars then Big T and I went upstairs to the room that we occupied and got high. I made sure I hid my stuff from him because when he gets high, he wants to clean and search for everything. My money was downstairs in a purse, tucked deep in the hall closet, out of reach.

I just had enough dope and coke out for us to use that night and to have to wake up on. The next morning, I got up earlier than I expected. I showered, dressed, and then headed on out to the park. I saw my longtime friend/sister, and she told me about a job at the stadium. I had to go to orientation and fill out paperwork then get an ID, and I also told Big T about it. He wasn't going to just be sitting on his ass reaping the fruits of my labor. No sir, he was going to earn his keep and help pay for where we were staying.

We got the job, and I was a cashier. I learned the prices really quick, and I was able to pocket at least two hundred to three hundred dollars on the days we had to work. I had to pay my niece, who was the runner and who also showed me the ropes. I also gave Big T something to hold him over until he got paid. Yes, it may sound crazy, but he had a tab with me. Nothing comes for free. Everything has a price, and I was beginning to realize Big T was a user. It never dawned on me that the men I had in my life were all takers, not givers. They each had a way of getting things from me, and me giving it to them in fear of losing them to someone else. I was slowly beginning to acknowledge the fact that I was my mother's daughter. As long as we can dished out, they stayed. When it all came to an end, so did the relationship.

I worked the stadium job for a few months, and then the gig was over. *What's next?* I was unable to provide money towards where we were staying, and her husband told us we had to leave their place. In the morning, I gathered what clothes I did have and went to see a friend on LeBaum Street. She had an extra room since her daughter no longer stayed there. She allowed us to stay for about a month and when I could no longer get her any alcohol, we definitely had to leave.

I was running out of thoughts and places to go, when Big T said we would go over to his sister's house. His sister and I got along fairly well, and she welcomed me into her home. It was uncomfortable at first because my only thought was, *Where am I going to get high at?* I knew doing it there would be a sure way to be put out. His sister was unaware of our drug usage, but she knew we drank and always had beer at the ready. After sipping on a beer, I had to go get high.

I told Big T I was walking to the store and of course, he wanted to tag along. He already knew what my *going to the store* meant. We walked down the parking lot and found an abandon building then went around to the back of it to get high. I always had water, syringes, cookers, lighters, stems, and chore boy with me at all times. I never knew who I may run into.

We smoked some coke and shot some dope then really made our way to the store. I had to have some chips, and he had to have a black and mild. When we returned, we stayed in the front for a bit, as not to alert his sister or her boyfriend. He called and told her that we were in the front, and she said the door would be opened. We finally decided to go in, after being outside for a couple of hours, enjoying our high.

We got situated and I nodded off no sooner than I sat down on the couch. Big T had made a pallet on the floor for us, but I wasn't ready to move just yet. His nephew entered the house, yelling and cursing. He was talking about why are we over here and I need to get up off the couch so that he can pull it out to a sleeper. He said that we were in his way. I snapped and I cursed him out then I picked up my belongings and left.

Big T came racing out to get me, and I was like hell no. I told him that his punk ass nephew would not be talking to me any kind of way with his young disrespectful ass. I really wanted to steal him in his face but like the little bitch he was, I just left. Big T's sister called his phone and told us to come back. I told him he could, but I wasn't. He asked me if I wasn't going back with him, where would I go.

I looked at Big T, and said, "Don't worry about me. I can take care of myself."

After I said that I walked away. I really thought he would follow me, but he didn't. That's when I knew that he didn't have my back like I had his. I hitched a ride back to the avenue, and the guy that picked me up got high. He asked if I knew where to get some dope from and did I have a place to go get high at. I said yes to both questions, and we were off.

One of the guys in the park had a place, and I already knew we could get in. The dude gave me one hundred dollars to go get some crack, and I did just that. When I returned, he wanted to know if I tricked. I looked at him and laughed. I told him if the price is right. He pulled out a stack of one hundred dollar bills and asked me if that was a good price? I looked at him with my eyes surely bugged out then I told him yep it sure was.

The guy from the park allowed us to rent his room because he knew he would be taken care of while we were there. By the time the sun came up, I had to have made about five more runs. He had given me three hundred dollars for myself, and I knew he couldn't do shit because his manhood never rose. It just lay limp on his thigh. He kept telling me to play with it, and I did. Hell, I was getting stoned, and I had a pocket full of money.

Whenever I made runs for people, they never got the full dollar amount. I skimmed off the package and pocketed money. I was a crackhead and a dopefiend. *Was I supposed to be honest and give them the full amount? Where in Southeast, did they do that at?* I asked myself and decided not in these parts.

I stopped fondling, and I started smoking more. I told him that I would be back because I had to make a run. I went and called the dopeman and got me a gram of dope. When I came back and dude was still smoking. He asked me if I would go to the ATM for him. *Duh? Would I? Hell yeah!* I thought to myself.

He had gotten real comfortable, and he was telling me that he was glad that he met me and he asked if we could hook up again. I told him yes we could. I took his phone number and he took mine then he gave me the bankcard along with the pin number. He asked me to take out two hundred dollars. What I actually heard him say was for me to take him out two hundred dollars and for me to keep three hundred dollars. After all, I was doing all the foot work all night and part of the morning. I deserved that.

I bought the money back to him then made another run. When we finished smoking, he said he had to be on his way and promised to call me later that night. That was fine by me. I walked him to the door and told him that I would see him later, and then he was gone.

I asked the guy whose place we were in if it was okay to shower and stay a little longer and he agreed. I gave him some money to go get some crack and some liquor, while I changed my clothes. I would be fresh dressed and ready to start all over again.

As I was putting my old clothes away in a bag, I noticed that I still had the bankcard.

Lucky me, I thought to myself. I wouldn't be able to use the bankcard until after midnight if the guy didn't realize I still had it. I sat at the table and gathered my crack together, putting some away until later then I started getting high and drinking. I was now out of cigarettes, and I decided to walk the few steps to the gas station.

When I got there, I looked over in the park and saw that Big T was there. He looked my way then I turned and went into the store. As I was coming out, he stopped me and asked why did I leave last night. I asked him why didn't he leave with me. He had no answer for me, and I had no answer for him either.

My phone rang, and it was one of my guys calling me for entertainment. That was the thing with me, I never identified with the girls who were out tricking on the street corners. I didn't consider myself a trick or whore. I was a paid call girl. People called on me to fulfill their wants, needs, and desires. I didn't have to stop cars and walk up to their windows to solicit sex. It wasn't until I went into treatment that I realized that I was a whore or a trick.

Now, as I was walking to go around the corner Big T wanted to know where I was going, and I told to take care of some business. He asked if he could walk with me and I told him that I was good. Big T asked if I was sick, meaning did I need some dope, and again I said I was good. He said he had something for me and I said okay as I continued to walk away from him.

I finally made it over to my friends' house, and he gave me an envelope with three hundred dollars in it, and all he wanted to do was to go down on me. That was no problem for me. I was still feeling wrong about it, but I needed to do what I had to do to keep my appetite for drugs fed. When I returned back to the park, Big T was at the table talking to his brother. I walked up, spoke, and then took a seat. His brother had been drinking and asked if I wanted a swallow, but I said no. I asked Big T what was up, and he said follow me. I wanted to know where we were going. He kept walking towards the alley.

When we reached a building, he stopped and asked me to cook up the dope. I was surprised he had anything after coming from his sister's house. I cooked it up and gave him his shot then I tied myself up and shot up. The dope was fantastic! I gave it a kick, and before I could push the blood filled syringe into my arms, I was headed into a good nod. I leaned my head against the wall and finally took the syringe out my arm.

Damn!

I hadn't had any dope like that in a while. I wanted that high to last a long time. I didn't even want to smoke any crack because it would've eaten up the dope. We sat in the alley for so long that I had to use the bathroom.

I told Big T I was going down the street, and as always he wanted to follow. I went to the back of the house I started from and used the bathroom. Afterwards, we all sat at the table and I pulled some crack out. I gave everyone some and just relaxed. I made a drink run, and when I returned I called the crack guy to meet me. I decided to buy an eight ball, so we wouldn't have to keep running back and forth. Big T surprised me by giving me forty dollars. I didn't ask him any questions on where the dope or money came from because I didn't want any lies. The truth would reveal itself in due time.

Big T received a phone call from his sister. He was trying to talk low and with my nosey ass, I was listening really hard. He walked out the door and I heard him say no I didn't take anything. I walked out into the hall, asking him was everything okay and he said it was a misunderstanding. He said his sister misplaced something, and she wanted to know if he saw it. That was a lie. He took her money and bought some dope then he gave me forty dollars. He bought some Black and Mild cigars, and now he was broke.

I went back inside and never spoke on it again. The night came in real fast and before I knew it, my phone was blowing up! The guy that I was with all night called. He said he would be over at about one AM, and asked if that was good and I told him yeah. Not once did he inquire about that bankcard. That struck me as odd. I wasn't going to offer any information.

I told the guy my friend would be coming over, and he didn't mind at all. This wasn't my place of residence, yet I was running it as if it was. Big T asked me who the guy was, and I told him that he was a friend. I wasn't ready to get into all those questions or answers shit. I knew I had money that needed to be made.

When ten-thirty PM rolled around, I decided to go to the store and get some alcohol. I needed to buy some new chore boy and two more glass stems along with a few lighters. I dropped them off at the house then went back outside. I stayed out until the clock struck twelve midnight then I went to the ATM to find out if any more money could be released.

I put in five hundred dollars and it dispersed then I got a receipt and it said the remaining balance was over five thousand dollars.

Damn!

I was going to be hitting that machine up and go shopping as long as he doesn't mention that card. Finally, one AM rolled around, and I received a call to come open the front gate that lead into the building. I walked down the flight of stairs and was greeted with a big smile and a big hug when I opened. I told him about Big T and he said he was cool with that. He didn't want any sex, he just wanted a friend and I was cool with that.

He came in and introductions were made. I pulled out some crack, the stems, and lighters, and I told everyone to go for it. Things were relaxed. We listened to music, danced, laughed, drank, smoked, and told war stories. We were having a good time. My friend passed me three hundred dollars and told me to make the call. I did and decided that my guy could come meet the buyer himself. That worked out really good. He actually spent another three hundred dollars with no questions asked. I would be able to hold onto my money and because of what he spent, my dealer gave me some money and some coke.

I put that up with my other stash and went back out to the front room. The liquor was still good and plentiful, so there was need to go to the bootlegger. I was so high that I had to go shoot some dope to come down. Big T joined me in the bathroom and when we came out everyone was still in their same place. The house man was feeling good, talking shit and nursing a bottle of Velicoff. I found myself sitting in a recliner by the window, staring into the darkness and nodding off. I could hear them talking, but I just couldn't respond to anything. I was stuck.

My friend said he was getting ready to leave because he had to go pack and prepare for a flight he had to be on by nine AM. He said he would call when he returned then I walked him downstairs. He gave me two hundred dollars and told me to take it easy. I closed the gate and went back upstairs. I was dead tired. I hadn't had any sleep in two days. My friend said I could take his bedroom, and I thanked him. In the morning I would talk to him about staying there for a couple of weeks.

I woke up well after noon, and Big T was already out the door and so was the guy I called my friend. He did leave the key so that I could lock up. I took out my works and some dope, cooked it up, and shot it. Then I took a hit of crack then went and showered. Once I came out and got dressed, I locked up the place and went to the park to give the keys to the owner and have a talk with him. We sat on the bench and I told him what I was facing. I told him that Big T and I had nowhere to go and I could assure him I would pay him for letting us be there. He didn't care too much about receiving money, but as long as he had a bottle of alcohol and a little smoke he would be okay. I agreed and made it all possible.

I went grocery shopping to stock the refrigerator and cabinets then I cleaned the house like it was mine. Big T joined in. We scrubbed the bathroom and bedroom then changed the linen and went to the laundromat. Everything seemed to be alright just for the moment. I went to the store and used the credit card to buy some clothes and shoes for me and Big T and when I made a withdrawal from the ATM there was less than one thousand five hundred dollars in there. I knew I had to withdraw that and juggle the money. I invested in some dope and began seeing some profit and continued flipping my money.

After two weeks, I hadn't heard from my friend. I wondered when he would return. I called his cell phone and it went straight to voicemail. I left a message for him to call, but he never did. The call I received was an unexpected one. It came from a police officer. They asked if they could talk to me and when would I be available. I asked them what was it concerning. They said an accident had occurred and they wanted to know if I could meet them at the hospital. I asked them why did they want to see me. They said my phone number was the last number dialed and they called me hoping to help the guy.

I went to Southern Maryland Hospital and was met by two officers. They asked me what was my relationship to the guy, and I said I was a friend. They asked me a lot of questions and I was getting tired of answering them. Finally, the police said my friend had been robbed and shot and was in intensive care. They said they found cocaine in his car and a glass stem along with a bottle of alcohol and a torn plane ticket. I was baffled. I asked if I could see him, and they allowed me to go in. He had tubes all in him and he looked really small compared to the guy I first met. He had no ID. He just had a phone with numbers in it and they would get around to calling all of them. I was still numb. *Who would do this to him and why?* I thought to myself.

Suddenly, I had a conscience. I was wondering why anyone would rob him when he'll give you anything you wanted or needed. Understand, this is coming from a girl who kept his bank card and withdrew money out then went shopping until the card was reported lost or stolen. I was a little pissed. I couldn't believe something like that would happen to such a nice fella. I left the room then went to the desk and asked the charge nurse if it would be okay if I left my information as the next of kin. She said that would be okay.

I left the hospital and was ready to go home and relax. When I got there it was trouble in the land. The guy whose place we were renting said Big T stole his food stamp card and exchanged it for money and we had to go. *Now what was I to do?* Big T said he didn't do it, and

I really couldn't be too sure of it because I knew him. I got my belongings and stashed them behind an old abandoned house then I sat on the back porch and got high. In the distance I could hear Big T calling my name, but I wasn't trying to be around him right then. I picked up my cell phone and called a girlfriend of mine and asked if she wanted some company and if I could stay the night with her. She told me that she had company, but to come on over. I got my little duffle bag and walked through the back alley to avoid Big T and get to her place.

My cell phone rang and it was Big T asking where I was and to meet him. I told him I was on my way to my sister's house, and that I would be there overnight. There was no need for him to ask if he could come because he knew the answer to that. I arrived at my friend's house and she gave me an upstairs room and a towel and washcloth. She told me that we would talk in the morning. I told her I had some dope and coke, and I asked her if she wanted any. She said that she was good, so I gave her twenty-five dollars and closed the door.

I sat there on the bed for a long time. I was wondering how I allowed myself to get back to where I said I would never go again. I loaded up my stem, took a hit then laid back on the bed. Suddenly, tears began to roll down my face. I couldn't fight them back. They just came streaming down. I wanted to get back on track but just didn't know where to start. I got up, showered then put on my night gown and smoked a little more. I promised myself that I would get some help one day.

The next morning, my friend and I sat at the kitchen table and talked for hours. I had to excused myself a couple of times because I felt a sickness coming on from not having any dope. I was in the room shooting up when my phone rang. It was Big T. I just let it ring. I was really getting tired of him as well. He was a leech, and taking more than he could ever give. I just wasn't happy anymore. I felt peaceful when I was away from him, yet I still was missing him. That was some crazy shit. My mind was screwed up as well as my life. I was so deep into the lifestyle that I couldn't see an outlet.

I made it back downstairs and told my friend I had to leave. I gave her twenty-five more dollars and promised to call later. I headed to the avenue where I knew I would find Big T and some dope. I had just took my last shot when I was at my friend's place. My stomach was bubbling and I was sweating and retching. I had to hurry up and get something in my veins.

I made it to the park and sent Big T to get three bags of dope for twenty-five dollars and two bags of crack for fifteen dollars. I walked in the alley and went under the porch of an abandoned house and got everything prepared for the dope when it arrived. Big T was back in like three minutes, and I was ready. I shot up twenty-CC's and was feeling real good. I gave Big T ten-CC's and then we smoked the crack, and I went in the park to play cards. Someone pulled up in a car and yelled out Big T's name and asked him to ride with him so he did. When he came back, he had some coke and dope which would keep us steady. I still had some money, but I wasn't letting him know about it.

My phone rang and it was a guy who wanted to spend some time with me and get high. I asked him what was he looking to purchase, and he said an eight ball and I called my guy. I wasn't in the mood to spend no time with anyone, so I knew how I was going to end this date real fast. I called around and got the answer I needed then I was on my way to that guy's house. The dealer would meet me there, and then we were going to rob him and leave.

I arrived, got comfortable, and poured myself a drink. He had a little coke on the table already, so I helped myself to it. He went in the room to get the money, and I watched closely to where he went so I could just smash and grab. It all worked out differently. I went in the bathroom and while he was in the front room smoking, I went in the closet and took out the shoe box. I grabbed the money, stuffed it in my drawers, and then went back out in the front room. My dealer called and said he was five minutes away and to look out for him. I said okay. I told the guy to give me the money so I could meet my dealer outside. He gave me the money and told me to leave the door unlocked. I said okay then I grabbed the money and went outside.

When my dealer arrived, I told him that the plan had changed then I jumped in the car. I told him that I would buy the eight ball and give him some money for just coming out to do that. When we got to his place, I went in the bathroom and took the money out. There was more than three thousand dollars. I gave him one thousand dollars and he gave me the crack and a ride back to the park. My phone was busy blowing up with texts and calls, asking me where I was and what's taking me so long. I dismissed it and went on about my business.

I went down the street to bag some rocks up and smoke some as well. I had the idea of sitting in this guy's house who was a smoker, and people came there to smoke, so I could make some money. The guy agreed and I gave him some crack for himself then he left the front room and I proceeded to bag up and get high. Before the night was through, I had made a little over four hundred dollars and I was glad about that. I called Big T and told him where I was, and he said that he would be down.

He arrived and still had coke and dope with him, which to me was a shocker. We got high then I laid back on the couch and fell asleep. When I woke up the sun was beaming high, and I had to get a move on. I left the guy with fifty dollars and some crack then told him I would see him later. Big T and I was walking towards the park when I heard someone yell there goes that bitch then shots rang out.

Big T and I ran through the alley and cut through some yards and ended up on Brothers Place, where we seemed to have lost the shooter. Before long, we were at the building we use to reside in and since I still had the front door key, we went inside and went to the laundry room. That was a close call.

Big T asked me what that was about and I told him I ran off with somebody's shit and now they were looking for me to get it or kill me. I also told him I took three thousand dollars from the guy. I never wanted to involve anyone with the mess I had made of my life, but Big T said he was there for the long haul. I never doubted that.

We sat in that building for over three hours talking and getting high then I suggested we leave. The next question was where would we go. We went back to the park and people were telling us about the guy that said he would be back, and I better have his shit or he would put a bullet in my head. That was life. Catch me if and when you can dude.

I called the guy's number and told him I was robbed and didn't want to come back empty handed. He asked why didn't I answer his calls, and I said I had just got my cell phone back. I said that I had dropped it when I was running. He asked where I was and said that he would come and get me. I told him not to worry. I was with family then I hung up. He called back and I answered, but this time I was crying like a baby. I could tell it was getting to him because he told me that wherever I was me would come and get me and that everything would be alright. He stressed to me that he wasn't mad about the coke and said that he could help me. I told him thanks, but no thanks because my family was sending me away to treatment. Lie after lie just flew out of my mouth. I would say things just to keep him at bay. He asked me to take down his address and to write him so he could send me a care package. I said okay then after that we hung up. Never were we to hear from one another again.

I decided I was going to walk on Mellon Street to see if one of the dope boys was out there. I called his number as I got closer and he said to meet him in the alley. When I walked back there, they were shooting craps. I leaned my back up against the wall and smoked a cigarette. I was just about through when he got up and asked what I needed. I told him three grams and he said to wait a minute. I watched him closely. I knew he kept his dope outside. I just didn't know where, but now I did.

I gave him the money and walked back the way I came then I wondered how long would he be out there. No sooner than that thought came to me, did I see him get up and run to the front. The other guys followed him then I headed back to where I saw him place his stash. I went behind the car then opened the gas tank and there it was. I grabbed it and ran off.

I got back to the park, and I didn't even tell Big T about what happened. That was his main man, and I had just stole his package. I made some phone calls and got rid of a lot. I still had my three grams to work with as well as some dime bags and a couple of half grams. Later that night, we knew we had to find somewhere to go. It was raining and neither of us had an umbrella, so we ducked and dodged through the alley and landed on the back porch of the abandoned house. There was cardboard there, so someone else must have been there and may be returning. That didn't bother us. We were ready to get high and settle down.

Laying on that cardboard with the cold rain splashing on us did us no justice. I had a thin jacket, but I used that to lay my head on. Big T stretched his legs out to allow me to put my head on him and cover myself with the jacket. We never really went to sleep. We were always worried about who would see us sleeping in an alley on an abandoned back porch. No one actually knew we were homeless. The last they remember was that we were waiting for approval on an apartment. That was a lie. We had no money and the money we got from robbing or stealing went for more drugs.

We got up, fixed our shots, and prepared for the day ahead of us. I was able to make some sales, since I was the only one in the park that early and they needed their fix before work. I sat on the bench and smoked some crack. At that point, it didn't matter where I shot dope or smoked crack. Everyone knew, so why hide it. The park police drove up as I was putting my stuff away and started patrolling the park. They were making sure there was no drugs or alcohol in the park. I had to go.

I made my way to the alley to get on my make shift bed and shot some dope. I nodded out for a good while because when I came to I had company. The people sitting across from me were strangers. They were telling me how they lost their place and had been living from abandoned building to the benches. I said I was sorry to hear that then I got up and left. This wasn't the time to make new friends. I didn't need people all up in my business.

I found Big T nodded out on the bench then I tapped him and told him I was going down the street to see if I could pay someone to take a nap. I was worn out from doing nothing. Getting high daily had become a full-time job with no real benefits. We went down to this guy's house that we called our brother. He was just a drinker, and he was gay. He used to say some real slick shit out his mouth to Big T until I had to put him in his place. I told him I would give him some money just to lay down for a while. He agreed. I gave him forty dollars, and he went on his way. Big T laid on one couch and I was on the other. We took a hit of coke, shot some dope, and then we went to sleep.

When we woke up it was almost midnight, and the guy told us we could stay the rest of the night. When we woke up the next morning, the guy sat in the front room and talked to us. He said he knew we had nowhere to go, and he invited us to stay for week. He said by then, we should find something or somewhere to go. We thanked him, and he handed me the spare key then we left the apartment. I was low on money and the dope was about gone. We had enough to get us straight to be out there in search of our next victim.

We walked in the alley, shot the last of the dope, and then chilled. Big T smoked his black and mild, and me a Newport then we nodded out. When I came to a fight had broken out. Then the bullets started flying. We jumped up and left. Luckily, none of the kids were injured. That park was always jumping with activity. We found comfort at our favorite spot in the alley. A friend of mine came walking through and asked if I had a glass and I said yes. She joined us on the back porch and smoked her crack. Big T and I used his glass to smoke what she had given me. My dope high was fading and I knew I would have to find some quick.

When she finished using my glass, she asked if I would be around. I said yes, and told her I'd be in the park since everything had died down. I sat at the table and smoked a cigarette, while the guys played cards. I called a spot, but by the time it was my turn my friend had come back and had some dope. I looked for Big T and he was nowhere in sight, so he would miss that one. My friend snorted so she did hers as she was walking. She just wanted to use the glass again.

I called my old childhood friend in the alley and asked him to watch my back while I shot that dope. My girlfriend couldn't watch me do it, so after she smoked she left. I cooked it up and pulled it in my syringe. I still had the few bags of coke she gave me, and I sat them next to me with the glass stem. I tied my arm up and shot the dope. Before I could get it all in me, I told my friend who was watching my back, damn this is the best dope I ever—.

Bam!

My head hit the wall and my eyes rolled in the back of my head. I was out for the count. He took the syringe from my arm and said he smacked me trying to wake me, but I wouldn't come to. He ran to get some help, but no one was there to help revive me. He called the paramedics and when they arrived, I was basically a goner. They had shot me up nine times with a drug called Narcan. It's used to reverse a opioid overdose. They were ready to pronounce me dead, but he said he begged them to do it one more time. The technician said okay and if I didn't come to this last time, he would pronounce me dead at the scene.

They gave me the shot and I began to come to. My eyes rolled around, and I didn't realize where I was. I looked on the ground and saw that my glass and coke were still there, and I quickly grabbed it. The EMT stated that he wasn't worried about that stuff. He just wanted me to go get checked out. I told him I was okay and they insisted that I go to UMC to get checked because my blood pressure had dropped tremendously. My friend E, was standing on the side, looking scared as shit. I asked him was he okay and he told me fuck no. He said that I was dead for ten minutes. He was yelling that he couldn't find anyone to help him or to help me. He didn't know where Big T had went. I cried and apologized to him for having to go through that. He begged me to go get checked. The dope I had shot had fentanyl in it. That was the same dope that had been claiming many lives all over the DC area.

I got in the ambulance and went to go get checked out. When we arrived, I signed my name in and waited to be called. In the midst of waiting, I noticed a group of policemen in the corridor staring in my direction. I looked at them and they were whispering amongst each other, then they proceeded to walk towards me. Call it paranoia all you want, but I do know that when the police get wind of an overdose, they want to talk to the victim if they survived. I was scared as hell. I wasn't going to tell them anything. I looked out the front glass window and saw that the A-Two bus was there. I made my way full force to the door then ran and got on the bus. The bus pulled off and I saw the officers looking around the parking lot. I ducked down in my seat and didn't get up until the bus was going around to Barnaby Street. I had a few dollars in my pocket, a glass stem, and some crack. I headed back to the park to search for my friend who had just gave me the dope that took me out. I never found her, but I did find another dope boy who let me get one for eight dollars.

After getting that shot up in me, I sat back and chilled to plot my next move. I got up and walked around the park then this girl bumped into me without saying excuse me. I asked her what was her problem, and she said I was. So me, being the egotistical person I am, I asked her to straighten it. She swung and I ducked. Just picture this, a dopefiend and an alcoholic in the park fighting over nothing. Each of us were throwing punches and rolling on the ground, tugging and pulling each other. She grabbed my hair and gave it a hard yank. I looked on the ground and saw a patch of my hair then I went ballistic.

The police came over. They broke us up, handcuffed us, and took us to their vehicle. The officer who grabbed me knew me from being in the park and always being high. He asked me a few questions and let me go with the promise I would stay out of trouble. I said yes, and then I walked away. The chick that started all this shit, gritted me up and down and mouthed off something. I looked and went on my way. I was filthy. I had to go shower and change clothes.

I walked down the street and when I reached the apartment, I realized I had dropped the key while in that scuffle. I walked back and searched the ground and when I was ready to give up, I spotted it. It was lying by a tree on an empty chip bag. I got the key and walked back down the street. Big T was still nowhere to be found. I went into the apartment and heard a lot of laughing coming from the bedroom, so I knew *brother* had company. I gathered some clothes and went in the bathroom to take a shower. I looked in the mirror and saw the patch that the bitch pulled from my head and was mad all over again. I stared long and hard at myself and didn't like the thin frail person who stared back at me. I was a stranger to myself.

I jumped in the shower and washed away all the events from the day and came out feeling refreshed. I lotioned down and put my clothes on. As I left out the bathroom door, I heard arguing coming from the bedroom. I just wanted to hurry up and get out.

Bam!

Something went crashing to the floor. I had just reached the front door when the bedroom door opened, and a thin guy emerged from the room. He had a cut on his forehead and was holding his side, which I noticed was bleeding. He asked me for some help, and I really didn't want to get involved. I opened the door and left without looking back. From outside, you could hear the fussing, cursing, and yelling. Then all of a sudden the front window broke and dude was hanging out of it.

The guy I called my brother was beating that dude to no end and it seemed like he was trying to shove him head first out the window. The dude was yelling and screaming, and I walked faster towards the park. When I got to the park, I finally saw Big T. I asked where he had been and did he know I had died from an overdose. I wanted to know if he even cared. Big T said that he had just heard about it. I was looking at him and asking myself, *Damn, why didn't you call to check on me or something?*

Big T saw the look in my eyes and went to hug me. I pushed him off and walked on up the street. For the first time in my life, I cried over a man I loved but one that never loved me. That was the second time in my life when I felt alone. I vowed that would be the very last time I would feel that way. I didn't need him. He needed me. In fact, I didn't even want that relationship anymore. That's what I kept saying over and over, trying to convince myself that I meant every single word.

I walked up to *Martin's Café* to see who was up there because I needed a fix. I saw the guy whose package I stole from the alley that was in the gas tank of the car. I asked him to front me one and he did. In fact he gave me two and said if I heard who stole his package to let him know and he would look out for me. He would never know it was me.

I left and went in the alley to shoot up, and Big T kept calling my name. I stopped and turned towards him then he was pointing down the street. The police were all over the place. The guy's house where we were staying was flooded with police. The police had him sitting on the ground outside. He was a bloody mess. He was crying hysterically and saying he was sorry and to just let him explain. I didn't want to see that dramatic bullshit, so I went on into the alley. Big T asked if I had enough for him and I said no. He told me to save mine, and that he had something for us.

No matter how hard I tried to get away from him, he seemed to always lure me back in with drugs. He knew I would not turn him down when it came to drugs. That was definitely my weakness. If it came in a small bag, I was bought. We sat on the back porch of a building and got high. The dope he had was good as hell. I wanted more of that. I asked him where did he get it from, and he said his man gave him something to try. The truth was Big T was selling dope for the guy, and then the guy would soon come looking for him and his money. I let that be right where it was with him.

I asked him was he going to have the man's money, and he said yeah. Big T said he only had two more to sell to have his money. With that being said this young girl was asking about some dope. She wanted three and he had two, so I gave up one of mine for the thirty dollar sale. She smiled and said she would be back and we both told her that we would be right where we were at. True to her word, she was back in less than thirty minutes. I told her to give me the money, have a seat, and I would be back.

She sat there with Big T while I walked back up to Martin's. I got four bags for thirty-five dollars and I only gave the girl two, telling her they were twenty dollar bags. They were healthy bags and she had no complaints. I had five dollars from the sale and another two bags to go with the other one I had previously. I wanted some crack. I was feeling real sluggish and needed a pick me up.

I managed to sell one bag of dope for nine dollars and with the five dollars I had thirteen dollars and got two bags of crack for that. I was tired from running back and forth and just sat on the swings and smoked my crack. I went to take another hit and the sirens of police cars scared the shit out of me. I dropped the stem and the crack and jumped off the swings. The cars weren't heading in my direction, in fact they were going down a whole different street.

I was stuck and paranoid as hell. I felt that they were coming for me. I picked up what was left of my glass stem and went in the alley, where I should've gone in the first place. I found my other glass and took the screens out the one that dropped and put them in the newer one then lit it up and the coke was still in there. A sigh of relief escaped my lips and the euphoria kicked in. The coke was so damn good, I could hear everything. I heard the people on the next block. I could hear people whispering. That coke had me feeling like I had a bionic ear.

I sat still, careful not to let anyone see or hear me move around. I was totally geeking. I began to look on the concrete to see if I dropped something, flipping my stem back and forth until it was bone dry. I was physically and mentally tired. I just needed to rest. I laid back against the wall and dozed off. I woke up to Big T shaking me. He was telling me that the police are canvassing the area looking for a guy who just bust off on someone by the Player's Lounge then ran down this way.

I picked up my stuff and scurried to the park and rested on a bench. I only was weighing maybe one hundred pounds and that's with the stems and lighters I carried in my pocket along with a bottle of Velicoff. I was totally washed up. I just wouldn't admit it to anyone that I needed some help before someone killed me or I killed my damn self. There was so many of my friends dying from alcohol and drug usage, I just felt it wouldn't be me. If I was going to die then it would be from the hands of someone else.

I continued to watch everyone as they came and went from the park. I especially kept my eyes on the drug boys. Watching where they put their stash of crack while they shot craps on the sidewalk. I knew I could make it to the curbside without drawing any attention to what I was doing. As they yelled out to each other, I made my way across the street. I lit a cigarette and pretended to talk on my phone. As I drew near to them, no one seemed to notice me standing there. I eased closer to the stash spot then dropped my phone, which allowed me to scoop up the package and walk away. I did it so smooth that none of them would have known I grabbed it even if they were paying attention.

I walked back across the street and headed to the alley. It was getting dark and I really just wanted to shower and lay back. I told Big T to follow me as I walked towards the brick building where we would go get high for the moment. My friend from the park asked me if I knew who had some crack, and I told her I had some. She wanted a twenty dollar bag and asked if I had another glass. I said no, but Big T allowed her to use his.

Before she finished the bag, she bought another twenty dollar bag and after she smoked it, she asked if I would be around and I told her yeah. She said she would be back in fifteen minutes. I waited and true to her word, she was back. This time she got a forty dollar bag and said that was it for her for a while. We exchanged numbers and said we would get up with each other the following day.

I used that money to buy a half of a gram and some alcohol because I knew we would have to have some drinks and money to give the old crazy guy we were staying with. When we left the store and headed to the house, we heard a lot of commotion from the park. They were fussing and arguing over some K-Two and some guy stabbed a girl. It was a mess. The park police made everyone leave and we went on in.

Crazy was sitting in the front room when we came in. He couldn't wait to tell us about what happened earlier that day and what the police said and did. Apparently, his lover of the day stole his money and bashed him in the head with a lamp, which explained the big gash across his forehead. He said the guy started calling him all kinds of names and he smashed his head against the front window, trying to throw him out. That shit got funnier by the minute because out of the room strolled his lover of the day that got his ass whipped. He was bandaged up, but still talking shit.

I told Crazy that I bought him some beer and a bottle of MD 20/20, and I also gave him twenty dollars. I showered then put on my pajamas and as they went back in the room, me and Big T smoked the last of the coke and shot some of the dope and called it a night. It was two AM when the door to the bedroom opened and they were arguing. Crazy woke me and Big T up and said we had to go. I asked him where should we go this time of morning. He said he really didn't give a fuck, just as long as we left there.

I was thrown for a loop. I had bought him beer, MD 20/20, and gave him twenty dollars, and still we had to leave. To top it off it had begun to rain. Not a heavy rain, but nonetheless, it was raining. I sat up on the couch, trying to make sense of this shit and just couldn't. I slowly got up, looked in the closet and grabbed my bag. I went in the bathroom to put my clothes on and took a shot of dope, wondering where would we go at this hour of the morning. When I emerged from the bathroom, Big T asked if I could give him a shot and I said let's wait until we left. He said okay and gathered his bag then we left. Before I closed the front door all the way, I had to say my piece to him. I called him every name in the book and told him he was a sorry ungrateful ass faggot who needed to be real and tell his friend he had full blown aids and is about to die.

The guy, all bandaged up, jumped from the room and asked me what did I just say. I told him that he heard me correctly and slammed the door as we left. That started another fight and I smiled as we walked towards the park.

CHAPTER SEVEN

We went in the alley, hoping to claim the back porch of the house, but someone beat us to it. We went to the playground in the park and I gave Big T the rest of the dope and I laid on the bench, while the rain fell down on me. It wasn't no ordinary rain. This rain was freezing cold rain.

I looked in my bag and pulled out an umbrella and tried to hold that while laying on that hard ass bench. I looked at Big T and told him that I can't do this anymore. He looked at me and shook his head as if he fully understood what I was saying. I cried and allowed the rain to mix with my tears. I asked God to just take me and do what needed to be done. I said I am so tired of living like this. Please help me! Please!

As I laid on that bench, being drenched from the rain, a small still voice rang out and told me that I've got you, my child. As soon as the sun rises, you will know what to do. I looked around only because the voice sounded as if it were right next to me. I cried some more, waiting for the first streak of light to hit the sky. When morning arrived, I was sick as a dog. I just needed one bag of dope to get me on my feet. As I walked aimlessly and bent over to the corner, I saw a dope boy, but I kept walking. When I was able to lift my head, the W-Four bus was pulling up. I told Big T I had to go and he asked where. I told I was going to P.I.W. I told him that needed some help and I thought that he should come with me. I thought that we could get clean together.

He rode the bus with me. We got off at Naylor Road and Alabama Avenue to catch the thirty bus to Wisconsin Avenue. That was one of the most longest bus ride that I had taken in a long time. I hadn't been on Wisconsin Avenue since I use to work at the Channel five building as a telemarketing rep, and now here I was going for detoxification.

When I entered the facility, I was greeted by a clinician, who asked me a lot of questions and registered me to be treated. He informed me that I would be there for at least seven days, depending on the level of detoxing I needed. I thought Big T was coming with me, but he didn't. He claimed that he was good and could stop at any given time. It was time for me to go upstairs to the adult psych ward, so I gave Big T a long hard look then turned and entered the elevator.

Once I entered the ward, I was given a room and asked to strip down so that I could shower and told that they would wash the clothes I had on. They gave me a pair of paper scrubs and that was what I was to wear while being there. The nurse said that once my clothes were done, I could put those back on. I left the scrubs on. I was sick to my stomach, so the nurse gave me a subutex, the generic form of suboxone, to help with the addiction of opiates. I took the pill and placed it under my tongue so it could dissolve, and a nicotine patch to stop the urge for a cigarette..

Moments later, I was feeling a lot better. I would receive two more before I went to bed. I decided that since I would be there for at least seven days, I could stock up on the pills and sell them when I got out. People were already selling their suboxone strips for eight dollars or better, so I knew I could sell the pills.

For the first two days all I did was sleep. I didn't want any food because I knew my body would reject it as well. The nurse bought me a couple of bananas from the dining room, and I managed to keep those down with lots of water. They said I was dehydrated and my blood pressure was quite high. I continued to rest.

The third day, I had to attend drug classes. I was bored out my mind, listening to those folks. I was given a doctor and he called me to go over my intake and medications. I asked him about visitors and he said he would allow me an hour visit. I called Big T and asked him to come up the next day and he said he would. The doctor wrote his notes and told me I was done. I left the office and went to take a shower and lay back down.

That evening at around dinner time, the unit team said I could finally go to the dining room and I went. I was looking around at all the food they had cooked and my stomach got queasy then I vomited on the floor. The janitor came out and cleaned it up, and I asked to go back upstairs. I had gone without food for so long that the smells were overwhelming, and I just couldn't take it anymore.

I went in my room and grabbed a subutex from my hiding place and took it then I laid back down. After a couple of hours, I was good to go. I went in the dayroom to watch television and guess who was in there, Dave Chappelle! *Damn, he came all the way to DC to get clean,* I thought to myself. When I got up closer, I realized it wasn't him at all. He sure as hell has a twin here in DC.

Me and the guy began to talk, and we found out that we were from the same part of town. We knew the same people and never once did we run into each other out there. I became his big sister and he became my little brother. We got along really good. He was released before me and we vowed that we would see each other on the avenue.

The next day arrived and so did Big T. The staff was saying I couldn't have a visit, and I kept telling them the doctor approved me for an hour visit for the day. They saw no notes in my file, and I went off. Big T was standing on the outside looking in and I was on the inside looking like a wounded puppy. I was in tears. I began to throw all the books on the floor and anything else I could get my hands on. They called the doctor and of course, he never answered. One of the staff members opened the glass door and let me go out to see Big T for about ten maybe fifteen minutes. I was upset because he rode all the way from Southeast to come all the way to

Wisconsin Avenue. He had spent about two hours on the bus. The staff member apologized to him and we said our goodbyes then I went on to my room.

The next morning when Dr. Doolittle came on the unit, I cursed him out. I called him all kinds of lying mf's and threw books at him.

He yelled to the charge nurse, "Give her forty of Halidol!"

I said, "I wish the fuck you would think of shooting me with that shit! I'll kill your ass in here!"

He asked the nurses to cuff me and put me in the padded room to allow me to calm down. *Like hell!* I thought to myself. I would not be treated like I was back in jail or prison. I went charging after him, and they shot me up then I went out like a light. When I finally came to, they were bringing me food. I tossed the Styrofoam tray to the side, laid in the corner and cried myself to sleep.

They informed me that I would be there another four days. Oh my goodness, it felt as if I was never going to leave that place. I needed to be on good behavior so that I could be released. I attended my classes and asked about getting into a drug treatment facility. I was told that since I didn't have an ID from DC, I wouldn't be able to get into a center. All I had was my North Carolina driver's license.

I talked to any and everyone who came in the door that was from a treatment center in hopes that someone would see past the ID and allow me to go in. If I didn't get into a program and fast, I knew I was going to use once I was released. I talked, begged, and pleaded with those people for a program, but nothing helped. The next day, I was to be released. I had nowhere to go but back on the streets.

I was bought downstairs to the lobby, and I received some quarters to catch the bus. I worked the front desk worker for several bags of quarters and when she left, I did the same thing to the next worker. By the time I finished, I had collected twenty-seven dollars. Before I walked out the front door, I yelled, telling them how I was going to ruin their name because they didn't want to help me get into a treatment facility and if I died out there, it would be their fault.

That's right. Just throw guilt in their face and it will change everything. Nope, not in this case. They asked me to leave the building or they would call the police and have me arrested. *Wouldn't that look good?* I thought to myself. A person who got discharged from their facility gets locked up and goes to jail because they were crying out for help. I wanted to see that happen. I was the type of person who doesn't believe that shit stinks unless it's smeared in your face. There I was, screaming in the building, cursing people out, being led outside so I could have my temper tantrum out there.

I told everyone who walked passed how that place wouldn't help me get the necessary help I begged for. I told them they just put me out on the street with nowhere to go. I just sat there and cried. I already knew if I went back to Southeast that I was going to get high and eventually die out there. This time if it wasn't from the drugs it would be from the hands of a drug dealer.

I sat there for about an hour and thought how bad I wanted a cigarette, only because I smelled it coming from the doorway. I walked over and asked if I could buy a cigarette and the woman gave me one. I lit it and walked towards the bus stop. The bus pulled up and I put the cigarette out then boarded. I tapped my SmarTrip and went and took a seat all the way in the back. I was tired, but I knew what I was planning to do before I even did it. I was going on the avenue and work that twenty-seven dollars and worry about what comes next.

The bus finally reached Naylor Road, and I got off and waited for the W-Four bus. I relit the cigarette and paced the sidewalk until the bus came. I made it to the avenue and it was a nice day for the month of October. The date was actually October 19th, 2014. I had been abstinent from drugs and alcohol for two weeks. My system was clean, and while I was in the detox center, I figured out how I could use and not catch a habit. This time I was going to be a functional addict. I was going to find a job so that I could get an apartment and not have to be on the streets or at anyone's place.

I looked around before I crossed the street. I was trying to see how I was going to spend this money and make it worth my while. I walked over to the park and everyone seemed happy to see me. I sure was glad to see most of them and to find out who had the best dope and crack around. I wanted some crack that I didn't have to recook and it comes back to nothing. I wanted some real melt down, sit me on my ass and geek the hell out crack. As I was getting the scoop on who had what, a lady I met and called my aunt had pulled up and got out her car then she walked towards me.

I asked, "Hey, Aunt Stephanie, how are you?"

She said hey, and then she told me that she was okay. She asked me what was I about to get into. At that time I saw three dope boys and the boy who had the best crack in Southeast walking towards the liquor store across the street. I wanted to reach them before they got away. I already knew I was going to get two bags of dope for fifteen dollars, one bottle of Velicoff for two dollars, a bag of crack for eight dollars, and four single cigarettes for the remaining two dollars.

She asked me again, seeing that my eyes were focused across the street.

I told her that I was getting ready to get me some dope and coke and a bottle of liquor and let that get into me. She said that she thought that I wanted to get into S.O.M.E. I told her how I had just got out of P.I.W., and couldn't get into a program because I had no ID stating that I was from DC. She said she could get me in. I was like, yeah, right.

Aunt Stephanie looked at me, and said, "If you're serious, I can take you there tomorrow morning, but you will have to go stay somewhere tonight and not use then I'll be there in the morning to pick you up."

She also said that if she found out I came back to the park that night, she was done with me. I said okay. I had her take me over my friend's house, and I stayed in. She left me her phone number and I gave her mine. I promised I wouldn't go to the park for anything. She left, promising me that it'll be better for me in the morning.

I couldn't wait for her to leave. She said not to go to the park, but she never said I couldn't call anyone to bring me something. I took my cell phone out and went to dial a number but my phone was dead. My friend told me to just lay down and see what happens. Give it a chance. That was all coming from a bonafide crackhead, who spent each waking moment getting high.

That night was one of the longest nights of my life. I mean, I actually went to sleep with some money in my pocket and woke up with some. That shit was crazy. That was another day that I didn't use. I took a shower and got dressed then waited on my Aunt Stephanie to appear. True to her word, she came and zipped me off to S.O.M.E.

The lady she spoke with told her to take me to APRA and then come back to see her. When I came back, we went it and gave her the paperwork then she said to give her a few minutes. We walked outside and stood by her car. That would be the start of a new life for me. I stood there and smoked a cigarette then they were calling for me to come back in. I walked in the building and was introduced to a program director, and she opened a door then told me to go in and have a seat. Just that simple, I was in the program I asked to be in. That would be the last time I would see Big T for a while. I was going to be heading to the mountains of West Virginia, after I got medically cleared to go. That day, October 20th, 2014, was the beginning of a new way of life for me.

I sat in a group which was called *Drop In*. It was a narcotics anonymous meeting for those in treatment or who returned from the mountains to get in an early meeting. There were some there who just went in to get off the street. When the group was over, I was told to go across the street to the safe house. Big T and Stephanie were still out there when I came out the building.

Stephanie was a graduate from the program and she was the angel that Allah sent to me to help me when I needed it the most. I told her thanks, as I made my way across the street. I asked Big T to bring me some cigarettes and he said he was going to do that right then. I never saw those cigarettes until I came back from the mountains. That's when I knew I had to leave him alone.

While in the program there are no relationships. There were a lot of them going on, but I was just mainly to myself. Everyone seemed to have their own clique in there, and I wasn't one to kiss ass, so it was best that I stay to myself. There was this one girl there from New York and she really thought she was the shit. She had her nose so far up her ass that you couldn't tell her shit. I had already heard that when at the safe house uptown was for both males and females that she had screwed one of the guys there. The guy thought he was a player. He would come through the door and act like he owned the place. He had got put out for having someone else's medication and tried to say he didn't know how it got in his belongings. These people were classic. Top notch bitches to me.

One day, as we got into the van to take us to the safe house, (they allowed the "older" residents to catch the bus) she saw her fake as boyfriend and whispered to him that she would meet him at the bus stop. She gave me this look, and I said what to her. She laughed and walked off. I called her a trick ass bitch and closed the van's door.

We reached the safe house before they did, and dinner was to be warmed up. I offered to help, but the young lady that was scheduled to do it said she was good. Cool. I got a cigarette out my pack and walked out back to smoke. Just then, tweedle dumb walked up. I asked her if she had a problem with me and if she did, we may as well settle it. The monitor heard us and had us come inside. I said my part and she just looked dumbfounded. I walked back outside, wondering if this program was going to be right for me. I knew that if I got into a physical altercation, I was done. I just wasn't the type to let anyone punk me down, be it male, female, young, old, cripple, crazy, etc. I was known to stand my ground.

The next day proved to be eventful. I got my first taste of recovery groups all day. It felt good doing something different, but my thoughts were back on Martin Luther King Avenue, wondering what T was doing and should I stay or go. I knew if I left, I wouldn't have anywhere to go, but if I stayed, I could eventually get my own place. I was just worried about Big T. *How was he making it out there? Where was he staying? Is he messing around?* Those questions alone stood out more than any other questions I could muster up to ask. I was lonely. I really missed the companionship. I was so use to being with and around Big T that I felt lost being here. I even felt guilty about being there. I felt that I should still be out there riding it out with him and as soon as that thought entered, Allah said, he wasn't there for you. He didn't want to get any help, but you did. Stay focused my child.

I shook my head and when I looked up, I realized everyone was gone outside on break to smoke. I had to just look around that room. That voice seemed like it was right there in front of me. They always said God talks to you, you just have to be still and listen. That was the second talk from The Man himself. I guess I needed to really be listening. I was told as a young child that God will reveal things to you, just be prepared to accept them for what they are. Slowly but surely, things were coming to light.

I saw a few people who would be on the avenue that knew both me and Big T. They told me that he was seeing his old girlfriend, and had been staying with her off and on. He would come to the park to buy dope for him and coke for them. I thought to myself, *Wow! That's why he couldn't make it up here to see me.* I saw another guy who asked me if I had received the cigarettes he sent to me. I told him no, and he said he gave Big T three packs of cigarettes for me then he told me to stay strong. He then reached in his pocket and gave me twenty dollars so that I could get a couple of packs and I thanked him. He pulled out the parking lot and I returned to the building for my afternoon classes.

The day went by pretty fast. I told the monitor a friend of mine gave me some money for cigarettes and she said okay, but the next time, they would have to come to the safe house to drop it off. I said okay and thanked her for her kindness. We were free to watch television or go for a walk. We all chose to walk and go to the playground. They even allowed us to go to the store. I bought two packs of cigarettes and some butter pecan ice cream. We watched the kids from Dunbar shoot hoops and we went to the other side to shoot hoops on the other court. We all were having a good time and that's when the New Yorker walked over to me and asked if we could talk. I said yeah and we walked off.

She said that she had no problem with me, and that she wanted us to be friends. I said yeah, okay, and then we went back to the bleachers. I sat there enjoying this end of October weather, eating my ice cream and smoking a cigarette. No longer did I have Big T to cross my mind. I made a conscience decision to leave him alone. Hell, he had already forgotten about me, so I said it's time to do me.

There was this one female that I knew from way back in DC jail. She was a whore back then and I figured that she had changed because she wasn't messing with anyone in the program. No matter where this chick went, she always had a girlfriend. She could never be alone. I was eyeing her for the most part, and my roommate who was also gay and had a girlfriend in the program, went and told her I liked her. She came over to talk to me and we laughed and joked around then in two weeks we were a couple. I told her about Big T and how he played me and that now I was on my own.

We had to be real careful about our relationship in there. If the wrong person finds out, we could be put out. I couldn't chance that, but I did. We decided we were going to be lover's and have a relationship while in the program. Remember I said I was lonely and needed companionship. I got just that with her. Being with a woman was nothing new to me, and I embraced those moments with her. When I was with her, I didn't have to think about the streets of Southeast, Big T, or anything else for that matter. I just was longing for the touch and feel of a body next to mine, and she provided me with that and more.

We spent a lot of time together, and I was wondering if anyone else knew of us being a couple. My friend for over twenty-five years came into the program, and she was placed in my room. She knew everything about me, and I held nothing back from her. She would even look out to make sure that the staff didn't walk in on us.

The time was nearing for me to go to the mountains. It was November, and we were going to have the Redskin's cook come over to S.O.M.E. and do a dinner for us. That would be right before Thanksgiving. I was told after the dinner, that I would be leaving the following Monday for the mountains. I begged and pleaded not to go. They told me all my clinical work was done and the doctor had signed off on my paperwork. Damn, I was getting ready to leave DC and my girlfriend.

They had already told her that she wasn't going to the mountains due to her psychiatric evaluation. I was dealing with a pure nutcase and she would show me real soon. That weekend, we stayed close to each other, promising to write each other and her promising to send me stuff. I told her don't make me any promises that she can't keep and she said she wouldn't and didn't. Sunday night, I began to pack my stuff up. I was given a large nylon bag to put my belongings in.

Since coming into that program, I had gained a lot of clothes and shoes and was starting to pick up some weight. My friend for over twenty-five years did my hair and I was ready to go. My girl and I stayed up the majority of the night, talking, holding each other, and shedding a few tears. I managed to get a few hours of sleep and before you know it, we were on O Street to face the beginning of our day. We went into Drop In and sat by one another and talked until the meeting started. The day was going by so fast. The van from West Virginia arrived, and we loaded our belongings then went to the dining hall to have our last meal together until I returned home.

We came out the dining room and I smoked a cigarette then we just stood there talking like the ninety days that I would be gone was a life sentence. I boarded the van and sat by the window then I looked out and began to cry. I was leaving my friend behind. *Isn't this how it was with me and Big T when I went into detox?* I asked myself. We waved at each other and blew kisses then soon we were out of sight of one another. I sat in the seat, pulled out a book and began to read. It was like a two hour drive from DC to West Virginia.

When new got halfway there, the driver stopped for a bathroom break and then we were back on the road. As we came to a spiraling wooded area, we began to say a prayer and I came to find out that was a ritual that had been going on for many years. We arrived safe and I was escorted to this big pretty house. It was called *Maya Angelou House*. The house was immaculate. No one would have ever thought that was a treatment house. The house had washers, dryers, pool table, nice sized rooms, a big kitchen, a large dining room, and a living room. There were bathrooms were on each floor and each room had their own bathroom with an adjoining room. It was nice.

Even though all my clothes were clean, they had to be rewashed and I was assigned a *buddy* who did all the laundry and made sure my room was ready and intact. I was able to go to the front of the line for meals for one week and I didn't have to do any chores. I was loving this resort already. We were able to go out and smoke all through the night if we chose to, and we could just sit out there and watch the moon, listen to the night life, and enjoy the comfortable weather. It had been a long day and I was ready to go to bed. I received my laundry and as my *buddy* carried it to my room, I proceeded to get ready to unpack it and get ready for bed. It was still early, but since coming in the program, I had begun to going to bed by seven PM and no later than seven-thirty PM. That had become a daily ritual for me.

After all my belongings were in the drawer, hung up, and shoes placed in the closet, I was ready for a shower. I left my pajamas on the bed along with a towel and washcloth then all I needed was to grab a bar of soap and I was ready. The shower was wonderful. The water coming from the shower head was beating down on my back, and I felt a sense of relief. Once I was done, I went downstairs to receive my medication, since they distributed to us and signed off on it.

I came back upstairs and went into the game room and played a few games of solitaire then I was ready to go to sleep. I can't remember getting back up. All I knew was that when morning came, I was feeling refreshed and ready to see what the day held. I washed my face, brushed my teeth, put clothes on, made the bed, then I went down the steps. Most everyone was in the common area watching the news, so I joined them. We were finally able to make introductions before breakfast. Someone yelled for Grace, and she never showed up.

It seemed that every time a meal was ready, they would call for Grace but she was nowhere to be found. I thought maybe she left on her own free will. It wasn't until a week went by, when I finally realized that when they called *Grace* it wasn't a person, it was to say the blessing before the meal. I was really beginning to wonder where Grace had disappeared to and why she didn't tell anyone she was leaving. Oh well, first lesson learned.

After breakfast everyone had a chore to do except me. I wouldn't have to do anything for a whole week, but it seemed so unfair. I asked if there was something I could do and one smart ass said yes, sit down. I stared her down and she looked at me and laughed then said enjoy your week hun, you'll get your chance real soon. The cleaning groups were done in teams with a team leader who oversaw all the work and signed off on it. If your chores were done, you earned play money, which could be used for movie night to purchase popcorn or even an outing into town.

The staff members came from the basement of the house and sat into chairs, while the residents sat on the sofas. Everyone went around greeting me and welcoming me, and then we started a meeting. Once we were done, we were given a recovery tape, paper and pen, so we could write about what we watched. My favorite movie has always been *Losing Isaiah,* so I could write a lot about that. When the movie was over, we did exercises with Richard Simmons, went outside to walk around, or went downstairs and got on the treadmill or bicycle. There was great motivation to staying healthy while recovering from drugs or alcohol.

Once exercising was over, we could ask the staff for a pamphlet to work on. The amazing thing was that these people knew about us and our needs before we even got there. They knew our behaviors, characters, flaws, strengths, and weaknesses. You could best say they knew us better than we knew ourselves. That was scary. No one would be able to pull the wool over these staff member's eyes. They were already hip to the game or games we played.

Next was lunch, then we had a little time for ourselves. We would go into step group and read and comment about the reading. It was great doing that. Just eighty-nine more days to go. I still found myself thinking of being back in DC. I thought of the ones I left behind, especially my new girlfriend. I sat outside wondering if this relationship was going to blossom or was it just for the time we were in the safe house. *Did I really like her that much to stay in a relationship with her or did I really want to go back to Big T?* The answer came the next week.

Someone came to the mountains from DC and bought me all kinds of messages of I love you, stuffed teddy bears, cigarettes, and an envelope that had money in it. I opened it up and it contained twenty-five dollars and a note that read: *I love you and I'm waiting for you to come back!*

That was so sweet that I actually cried. I didn't ever receive a note, cigarettes, teddy bear, or anything from Big T while I was in the mountains. Therefore, he was dead to me. She even left me a phone number to call her, and I was going to do that Sunday. I was going to make sure I gave her the phone number there also. We kept in touch the whole time I was there. There wasn't a weekend that I didn't talk to her.

Two weeks later, someone else came from DC and told me that she was being put out the program and the staff drove her over to Franklin Street Northeast, which was her old drug area. I began to worry. *Was she back using again and did she go back to her old girlfriend?* I was in West Virginia and I couldn't get to DC. unless I decided to leave or get a doctor's appointment. I chose the latter. I complained of migraines and also asked to see the psychiatrist. Appointments were made and I would be in DC within a week.

I called her on Sunday to inform her I was coming to DC, and I received no answer. My mind began to race and it was telling me all kinds of shit, and I made a conscience decision to leave her alone as well. It seemed like everyone had a game and my patience with people was wearing thin. My trust level was low and I was ready to cancel my appointment, but I knew I had to go since it was made. I sat in the van looking like a lost puppy.

We finally hit DC and before I knew it we were on O Street, getting ready to park the van. I got out the van real slow and when I started walking to the safe house, I heard my name being called. I looked and there she was. I know I had to have been grinning from ear to ear. If staff never knew about us then, I was sure they knew now. It was obvious. I couldn't run to her and hug her like I wanted to. I just waved and said I would be over to the main building in a few minutes.

She was waiting patiently for me. Everything I planned to say to her went away. I knew right then and there that we were going to be together. She went out of her way to make sure I had all the things I wanted or needed while in the program. I just couldn't form the words to tell her that we were done. I decided to actually see where that would take us once I was done, and I would be able to spend time with her outside the program. She was such a caring person. She looked out for any and everybody. They use to call her the *candy lady* in the morning group because she would always have a pocket full of candy. That day she had Reese's cups for me, cigarettes, and money. She said the next female to come up, she would give them soap, deodorant, and toothpaste for me. I told her not to worry about it because they supplied us with hygiene/feminine products, but she still sent it by the young lady. I was thankful for and very much appreciative of everything she was doing for me. She even said she also had a phone for me. I just grinned like a school kid. She was a warm and lovable person, just needy.

I wasn't sure how this was going to play out. It was time to head on back to the mountains. She said she would call me early Sunday, and I said okay then I boarded the van. December rolled around really fast and so did my birthday. They made me cupcakes. All the other residents sang *Happy Birthday* to me, and we enjoyed ourselves for the moment. The next day I put in an application to attend CET, which is a training center that S.O.M.E. has for residents who wants to get into the medical field or HVAC. I wanted to go for the medical administrative assistant program.

A couple of weeks later, I received a test and was told to send it back within a week. A staff member took the letter to the post office and I waited patiently to hear back from them. That afternoon when we had group, I finally wrote a *goodbye letter* to my mom. I read it out loud, put it in an envelope, and buried it in the mountains. I was ready to heal from the hurt of not being there for my mother and I held on to a lot of shit for years. It was a relief and my God mom was there with me through it all. I cried, but this time I knew I was being freed and freeing my mother as well.

Within the next couple of days, staff took us to pick out a tree. We picked out a beautiful one. When we got it to the house, we could hardly wait to put it up and decorate it. Christmas eased around, and when we all woke up the tree had a bunch of gifts under it for us. We were all shrieking with laughter and joy at the many gifts that was there for us. We had a great dinner that night and went to bed full and awaiting the next day to come. I knew I had less than forty days to be there, and I just relaxed. It was smooth sailing from there.

The months passed and it was time to do my relapse prevention plan. I had to do two scenes of making a plan to escape when confronted with the idea of getting ready to use, and one on actually relapsing. I hated that scene. It was as if I actually used. Playing it out with other residents made it all seem so real. I cried and lunged out at a staff member, and they had to comfort me and tell me that it was okay because I didn't use. I knew right then and there that I was going to be in the *No Matter What Club* for life!

It was nearing my departure and it was a matter of using the tools the program taught me, so I could stay on the straight and narrow. I received the letter from CET, and they said they couldn't wait to meet me. I met all the requirements to be in the MAA class of 2015! Before I knew it, I had one week left and I was starting to get nervous about returning to DC. If West Virginia had a transitional house there and available jobs, I would have stayed there. No joke. I would've stayed in touch with my friend and probably asked her to consider moving to the mountains.

The day before I was to leave, the staff put out an eviction notice, saying it was good having me there, but it's time to go. Everyone signed it and I placed it in my keepsake folder to keep with me. The ladies helped me load my belongings in the van. It's amazing how I went up there with quite a bit of stuff and left with three large army bags and two duffle bags full of shoes.

*****

We all hugged and said our goodbyes and see you later, and then I was on the van heading to DC with another female who I just couldn't shake from being around me and a couple of guys. This one guy talked from the time we got on the van until we were back in DC unloading the van. I was so glad that they dropped us ladies of first. This was the first time in a long time that I was tired of hearing someone talk. Damn, he was a mouth all mighty, tongue everlasting, talking ass dude. See you later, not.

We made it to the Harvest House, which was the transitioning house for women. The women there were like two groups ahead of us, but nonetheless, we all got along. I met with the staff of the house and was told which room I would be in. I was glad to have a large room, and my roommate worked and we got along fine. I was her Goddaughter in the mountains and now we were together again. The day finally came for me to go to CET and fill out the necessary paperwork and take a urine test. This was going to be a cinch. I was eager and ready.

Two weeks later, the director called and told me I was accepted into the medical administrative department, and that I didn't have to worry about wearing scrubs right off. I would be in casual clothes for two weeks then it would be scrubs. The program was designed for up to six to nine months. I finished in five and a halfmonths and took my certification and when I went on my externship, I was hired to work at the doctor's office in the big chair. It was a glorious opportunity, and I was real happy to be doing something constructive.

Now it was time to really put all the tools I learned in the program to work. I've always been a stickler for time. If you're early, you're on time and if you're on time, you're late. I made that my motto and it worked. I would arrive at my place of employment by six-thirty AM no later than six-forty-five AM to turn on the eye machines, make coffee, and turn on some gospel music to set the tone of the office. Since I was the first point of contact, I set the tone of the atmosphere.

There were many disruptive patients that would come through, and I would have to hold back from going off on them. Patients would be on their cell phones, and when you tell them no cell phones are allowed in the office, they would get loud and ghetto. Remember, this is the Southeast office I worked in. The doctor I worked for, also had an office uptown in one of the hospitals where I would also go to work on certain days. There's a big difference in his offices.

The Northwest office was laid back. The people were cordial and listened. The Southeast office was bonafide ghetto! People always wanted to fight and do whatever they chose to do. When you asked them nicely, they still got mad. Most times, we would have to cancel their appointments then call their insurance company and explain what happened and why we could no longer see that patient.

I basically stayed to myself. There was this one young lady who showed me all there was to know about doing insurance. I was so sad to see her go. The other young lady always seemed to have it out for me. We got into heated arguments quite a few times, and of course we were sent to the office manager's office. I really wanted to get this girl off my back, so I figured the best way was to fight her. I called my CSW and told him what was going on and he said it was because I was new and catching on fast. People will feel threatened when a *newbie* comes in. We never got into that fight I so desperately wanted. I let her be, and she let me be. She was sneaky as hell though. She would find anything I did, and run behind my back and tell upper management. She was a thorn in my side. I just had to ignore her and do my job to the best of my ability.

While working, I was still in the transitional home and it had been a year. After using my extension up, they found another place for me to go because there were no vacancies for a S.R.O. (Single Room Occupancy). I then entered *Calvary Women Services* located in SE. It was good for me because my job was right around the corner. I didn't have to worry about a bus or anything, and I was glad it was convenient. After four months of being there, my one year clean anniversary was approaching and I couldn't believe that I have actually not had a drink or a drug in one whole year! I celebrated my anniversary in the S.O.M.E. dining room. It was a great celebration for me because my dad showed up. He could finally set eyes on his first born who was now free from active addiction. He hugged me so hard and told me how proud he was of me and we cried together. I returned back to Calvary House brimming with so much love that I received from the people in the rooms of N.A.

A few weeks had passed and a bed finally came up for a S.R.O. I immediately called my CSW, and he came and helped me move my belongings. I was about to have my own room and not have to be worried about my stuff coming up missing. The program director called me and allowed me to do a walk through. I had an end room, so it was huge. It was like having two rooms in one. The room had a single bed, two dressers, a chair, a mini refrigerator, and a nice sized closet.

I told her yes I wanted it and we immediately started the process. I moved in around November and my CSW helped. I called my girlfriend to tell her the news and instantly, she wanted to come over. I met her at Anacostia Station and we rode the A-Eight to my new place. I was on the third floor and those were some steep steps. When we went into the room, my girlfriend hugged me and told me how proud she was of me and for me to keep doing *the damn thing*! I have to admit, I was proud of myself. We went in the kitchen, which was shared by other residents and I cooked us something to eat. This was going to take some time getting used to, since I was use to the staff waking me up at a certain time to get ready for work.

My friend gave me the cell phone she said she had for me, and I was glad to have my own cell phone at last. Because of my work schedule, we had to say our goodbyes and promised that we'd see each other in a couple of days. That would be the weekend, where she could stay a little later, but be able to leave on time to get to her residential living place.

My birthday was approaching and I would be turning the big fifty! I got on my knees and thanked God that I would actually see my fiftieth birthday clean and sober. I met my friend at the park the next day. I wanted to play some cards and see what the people had been up to while I was gone for a year and some change. The majority of the people I had got high with had passed and those who didn't were doing the same old thing. I sat there at the bench looking at all the old faces and the new ones and thought about how I looked when I was in my addiction. I had a big bobble head with a small body looking like a chocolate blow pop. I thought I was finer than wine and no one could tell me any different.

That day was different for me. I was weighing two hundred and eight-three pounds. That was a big difference from the ninety pound girl who went into treatment. A lot of people were glad to see me, while others rolled their eyes. I laughed because I knew they didn't have the courage to say anything to my face whether I was clean or using. Everyone who knew me knew I would curse you out or fight you if it came down to that. I wasn't a bully. I just didn't stand for a lot of crazy nonsense or foolishness. If you talked shit about a person, be ready to back it up.

I was so caught up with the park that my old dope dealer touched my shoulder and asked me to walk with him. We walked over to the gas station. I got a cup of ice and a bag of Martin's Red Hot Chips. He said he found out I was the one who stole his stash in the alley from the gas tank of his car. I neither confirmed nor denied it. What he said next threw me for a loop. He told me that as long as I stayed clean I didn't owe him shit. He also told that the first time he heard of me using or saw me using he was coming for his payment. I just looked at him. He gave me a hug and told me he was proud of me and to stop hanging in the park.

I went back over to the bench and thought about what he said to me. My friend and I said our goodbyes and walked across the street to board the bus to go to my place. When we got there, we sat on the front for a while then went upstairs to watch some movies, eat, and talk. I had been hearing that she was talking to a female in the house where she stayed and she kept denying it. I told her if I found out differently it's not going to end well. She laughed it off.

The following weekend was my birthday and I wanted to spend it with the ones I loved. My sponsor, my dad, and my girl. I went to the movies. That was the best time of my life. Just to have my dad back in my life. My dad had told me that he wasn't in the best of health and said he took his medicine but not like he should. I begged him to take his medicine and he said he would do his best. My sponsor took my dad home then he dropped me and my friend off at my place, and we all said our goodbyes. I stayed outside with my friend for a while and when the bus came, I went on upstairs to my room.

I took my shower and by the time I was ready for bed, she called. There was a lot of noise in the background of her cell phone. I asked who was that yelling in the phone and she said the female's name. I asked if that isn't the same girl they told me you're messing with and she said no. Here is where all the lies came tumbling down. The girl was apparently yelling at her and she was trying to keep the girl quiet. I hung up and she called right back. I just let the cell phone ring and go to voicemail.

The next morning, she called my cell phone and again I ignored it. As I traveled to work, all that confusion from last night was on my mind. I had to shake it off. I got to work and made a cup of coffee, talked to the doctor for a minute, and then he prayed over me and for me. Lunchtime rolled around and when I went outside to smoke, there she was staring me in my face. I confronted her again about what went on the night before and she still said it wasn't about her. I told her I would see her at the meeting that evening.

I finished my shift, clocked out, and then went home to shower and change clothes. I would have to catch two buses, so I kind of rushed myself to get out the house by five-forty-five PM. Once I reached Anacostia Station, the ninty bus was there and I boarded it, heading uptown. During the whole bus ride, my cell phone rang with my friend on the other end. I finally answered and she told me that she was running late, but would be there a little after me. I said okay and hung up.

By the time I got to the meeting, I was able to help set it up by putting the literature on the table along with the readings. The room started filling up, and the meeting was ready to start. There was no signs of old girl. I put my cell phone on vibrate and paid attention to the speaker for the evening. By the time the secretary's report came, my friend still had never showed up. When the meeting ended, I tried reaching her but received no answer. I left numerous messages and all were left unanswered.

When I got home, I called the payphone where she resided and asked to speak to her best friend. When she came on the line, she already knew what I was going to ask. She answered me truthfully and asked me to call her on her cell phone. After I took her phone number, I immediately called and she answered all my questions that I already knew what the answers to.

The whole time that bitch had been lying to me, but I was going to play it cool with her. What I just heard had actually made me sick to my stomach. My friend had taken this chick to a motel and had given her three hundred dollars to get a coat. *For real?* I thought to myself. Sunday rolled around and she had called me a little after one PM. I asked her what happened to her and why she didn't come to the meeting. She said she had an emergency with her daughter, and they had to go out to Virginia to help her mom out. I just listened as she dug the hole a little deeper. She said she wanted to come over, and I asked her to meet me at the park. When I got there, I saw a girl I called my sister. We used together back then, and she was also getting herself together. She told me she was in a transitional house. I asked her where and when she told me, I told her my girl also lived there. When I was about to say the name, my girl walked up and this look crossed both their faces.

I asked them do ya'll know one another, and they both looked dumb while shaking their heads no. I knew differently. I'd been in relationships with enough women to know when their lying, and they both were lying. *How could you not know a person living in the same building? I* thought to myself. I let her believe I was stupid and I walked away. My friend kept calling me and when I turned to look her way, I heard the words see you later escape from her lips to the girl I called my sister.

I smacked the shit out of her and told her to get out my face before I caught a case. A few of my friends came to drag me away from her, and I left her standing right there looking at me walk away. I went home and cried. I was really hurt. She was the one person I actually believed in when she told me she wouldn't be like all the others who hurt me. I had found comfort in her and now I was alone again. I knew I couldn't be with her sexually anymore because she had been with my so called sister. The fact of her just being with someone else made me even more mad and ready to fight her.

She kept calling me and I answered only to tell her to come get the cell phone and that we were done. She said she was sorry. She told me she felt neglected by me and that's what made her do what she did. My friend, who I had put my trust in and opened up my heart to, had betrayed me. I just couldn't understand any of that. I didn't want to understand it.

I went to work the next morning, and she walked in for an appointment. I was the only one at the front, so I had to gather all her information and log it into the computer then get a copy of her insurance card. I actually had to be nice to her after what she had done to me. I had to realize that I was on my job, and she was our patient. Once she did her screening she asked if I could step outside for a minute after I checked her out of the system. I did.

All she kept asking me was to forgive her and give her another chance. She said she didn't know that girl was like a sister to me and I told her whether it was a sister or not, she cheated. My now ex, asked me to keep the cell phone, and she would continue to pay the bill. I told her I could pay the bill but she insisted, and I allowed her to do so.

She would call me every day to ask how I was doing and if she could come over. The day I allowed her to come over wasn't a good day. I met her out in front of my building and I sat there for a minute and smoked a cigarette, trying to figure out why did I agree to let her come over. It was obvious. I wanted revenge on her. I wasn't on some get back shit, I just wanted to beat the hell out of her and that's what I did when she got into my room.

I took her cell phone and threw it to the floor then smashed it. I began to punch her in the face, and I threw blows to her body. I grabbed her and smashed her head against the door and kept asking her why. I asked her why did she do that to me. I wanted to know if I deserved that. She cowered over and laid on the floor with her mouth bleeding and clothes torn up. I just sat there and smoked a cigarette while she tried to get herself together. Every time I looked at her I wanted to punch her some more.

I kicked her and told her to get the fuck up and get the fuck out. I told her not to ever call or come to my job again. She continued her pleas of being sorry, and I was really tired of hearing them. I got up and walked her downstairs and opened the front door to let her out then I went back to my room and cried. It was over.

I went about my days feeling lonely and lost. I continued going to my meetings and whenever she showed up, I sat further to the back then left before she would know I was gone. I hurried up the street to get on the ninety bus to take me to Anacostia so I could get on the A-Eight and get home.

My days seemed to be longer than usual. I was getting off work, coming home to shower, and then going to bed after I took my meds. I hadn't eaten in a week. The only thing I had was coffee and sodas to keep me full. I didn't feel like cooking anymore. I was indeed missing her but I knew I had done the right thing by letting her go. I figured I wasn't the one for her and hoped that she would find someone she would be true to.

*****

Months had gone by, and I was told my dad wasn't doing too well, so I decided to go visit him. He seemed so small and frail. Mind you, my dad wasn't a big guy at all. He was tall, slim, and bowlegged. I would say his height was around six foot two inches or so. He had facial features the of Eddie Kendricks from the Temptation. He was the smoothest man I have ever known. To see him in his bed all small, I couldn't erase that image out my mind.

My dad asked me for a cigarette. I didn't know he wasn't supposed to be smoking, so I gave him one. My sister said he's not supposed to have that, and when I took it from him he gave me a look like aww man, really. I him that he knew he wasn't allowed to be smoking. The sadness from his eyes depicted the look of a wounded child. I even started feeling bad for taking the one thing away from him that he wanted the most.

My sister and I began to fluff his pillows and realized that he had been hiding his pills underneath them. I shook my head and told my aunt what was going on. She asked me and my sister were we able to come over some days and assist with him. Because I was in a program and still had guidelines to follow, it would be impossible for me to do so.

My sister and I fed him and my uncle, gave them their meds, and then washed the dishes up. When my aunt came home, we left. My father's birthday was approaching in June, and he was taking a turn for the worse. My dad had his seventh birthday on June 16th, and it was celebrated at his bedside. I was watching my dad fade away. That wasn't supposed to be happening.

My mother was gone and all I had left was my father. He was supposed to be here to bury me. I had no one else left. On June 20th, I received a call saying that I need to be at the house. I went reluctantly. I really didn't want to see my father like that. *What could I do to make it better?* I wondered to myself. Nothing at all. When I left there, heading home, I felt defeated. I asked God, why take my dad. Take me please. I felt I wouldn't be able to go on without him. *We had been estranged for so long and now that we had each other, why would he leave me so fast?* I thought to myself. I had a lot of questions and they would go unanswered.

June 24th, I decided to take a trip to the park to see what was going on and to take my mind off my dad. I got off the bus in front of Popeye's and decided to get a two piece meal with a drink. I walked over to the park and sat down at a bench by myself to eat. I was placing my keys on the table and they fell to the ground. I bent over to pick them up and there was a bag of dope lying under the keys. I picked the keys and the dope up. I held that little bag in my hand, playing around with it. The whole time I was looking around for someone who may have some works.

I ignored the food and concentrated harder on finding a way to do that bag of dope.

A very clear voice asked, "Really? You're going to let that bag take you for everything you worked hard for."

I looked around because surely someone was talking to me. No one was around me, and no one saw me pick up that bag of dope. It dawned on me then that the voice came from someone mightier than a person in the park. It was God himself.

I then saw this guy who sold dope and I went over to him, and said, "Look, I don't know if this dope is yours or not, but please, please take this from me before I do something really stupid!"

The guy took the dope then looked at me, and said, "If I wasn't sure about you getting clean, I am now."

He told me the look on my face told the whole story. He said there were many people in the park that were betting against me. They were just waiting for me to slip up. I shook my head and walked back to my food and cried while I ate. Later that evening, my cousin took me to see my dad. He had a tube up his nose and his eyes were half opened. He had a cool rag over his forehead.

My nephew and I stood by one another as we watched my father, his grandfather, start to transition. It was not a good feeling watching someone getting ready to die. My nephew left the room and I followed. We went into the dining room and my aunt wanted us to start helping her get his affairs taken care of. We were to call doctor's to cancel appointments, Social Security, Medicaid, Medicare, and whoever else that needed to be contacted

Everyone being emotionally drained, said their goodbyes then went home. On June 26th, we all gathered again. The hospice nurse was there and she told us that hearing was the last thing that goes. I had a moment with my dad, and I told him that I loved him and appreciate him so much. I thanked him for the tough love I received while being in the program. I told him I was okay and if he was ready to go that I would be okay. I promised him I would never go back to drugs, and I told him how I almost slipped up because I was losing him. I told him that my brother, sister, and nephew would be okay. I gave him a kiss on his forehead, his cheek, and then gently on his lips.

I left the room and told my cousin I was ready to go. Later that evening, at seven-forty-eight PM my dad passed away. I really thought I was going to lose my mind when I got that phone call. As my aunt prepared the arrangements, I tried to busy myself at work. I informed my job that my dad had passed, and I received a little time off. The day before the funeral, I went over to my aunt's house where my dad had lived for so long, and spent the night to get ready for the services the next morning. I tossed and turned and when I walked pass his room, I would cry.

I was crushed and I knew my aunt was as well, after all, she was his caregiver and to watch her brother pass away was too much for her. My aunt did a lot for her brother. She had to not think of him as her brother and use her nursing skills in order to get through bathing him, changing his bed pan, and his Depends. She also had another brother that she cared for and also had to do most of the same things for him. My father was being cremated, but we will still have an open casket funeral. The pastor from the church I attended performed the eulogy and my cousins did a praise dance in memory of him.

When the casket closed that's when I lost it. My dad was really gone and would never be back. I tried to control my tears, but they continued to fall. Once the services were over, I went back to my sister's house where the repast was to take place, and then we found out my cousin was having a repast over her house as well. None of us knew that was happening. It kind of threw us for a loop. I sat with my sister for a while, then my cousin and I excused ourselves. She dropped me off at home, asking me if I would be okay. I promised to call her then I went in the building and straight to my room. If ever I needed someone in my life, at this time and moment that would have been perfect.

I took my shower, took my medication, and then I fell off to sleep. I can remember waking up throughout the night, looking for my father then crying myself back to sleep. My sister had got necklaces that could hold ashes and gave them to me and my brother and she and my nephew had one as well. I asked my sister to place it around my neck and vowed that it would never come off.

One day I was sitting at work then I went to turn the hook part of the necklace towards the back and it fell from my neck. Ashes were in front of my shoes and I immediately began to scoop them up to put back in the container around my neck. One of the doctors asked me what I was doing, and I explained what happened. She was so insensitive. She told me that the dead can take care of their own. I gave her a look and told the other doctor, whose office it was, and he had a talk with her. She came to apologize to me, but I was stung by her words and wanted nothing else to do with her.

Everything I learned in the program was about to leave me at that moment. All I wanted to do was leave, and I was granted permission to do so. I thought about putting something in her gas tank as I was leaving, but I prayed about it and let God deal with it. It had been almost a year and I still wasn't ready for a relationship. I began hanging at the park more and more, not caring what anyone thought. I was a grown ass woman, and I could make my own decisions.

I was up there one day and one of the staff members from the house I lived in honked her horn to get my attention and ask me why was I up in the park. I told her because I can go anywhere I choose to as long as I'm not using, but they saw differently. I met this guy up there and we would generally play cards together as partners then things went another way. We started seeing one another, but it only lasted a couple of months because he was a weed head and I just couldn't deal with that smell. He had to smoke blunts one behind the other.

One night he came to visit me and had smoked a blunt in his car on the property. I was given a urinalysis test because you are the company that you keep. Now I understand that saying very well. He worked security for different singers and bands, but it would always seem like he stayed broke. He asked to borrow three hundred dollars from me, and I didn't hesitate to give it to him. I even rode with him to the weed man's spot to cop.

Was this going backwards in recovery? For me, I didn't think so as long as I didn't pick up and use, I would be okay. It took him forever to pay me back. He was paying me in installments. He would give me forty dollars here, twenty dollars there, and so on. He still owes me forty dollars, but fuck it because I'll never get it. We only had sex twice, so I didn't allow my feelings to get involved. It was actually what I called *make me feel better sex*.

That ended as quick as it began, and then I was back alone. I really had no problem being alone. Being alone meant I didn't have to worry about anyone else but myself. I could do that. Months went by and I became more engrossed with my work.

*****

This young man who was a patient walked in. He was on his cell phone and had a bottle of water in his hand. He was talking loud on his cell phone. I looked at him and got his attention then I informed him there's no eating, drinking, or talking on a cellphone allowed in our office. He asked me what could he do and I told him to have a seat and wait to be called on.

He said you keep saying something to me, so you must want my number. I looked at him, smiled, and said to him, Mr. Brandon, if I want your number all I have to do is look in the system. He told me well use it then. I laughed it off. Friday came, and I saw him in the meeting I attend and we spoke. I believe I gave him my phone number and called the next day. We talked and he said he had a friend, and he was just trying to see where it was going which was a lie. I told him I had a friend, but actually we were done. Neither one of us wanted to come clean with one another, so we just played our little game. I had bigger fish to fry.

I enrolled in the escrow program to help me save money. I was determined to get a car. I called my play sister, who drove me out to a dealership that was advertising, seven dollars down and you could drive away with a car. Liars! We drove there to hear all the lies then we left. I was disappointed, but knew I would be okay. I called my female sponsor, who drove me to *IAD Auto* in Maryland to get a vehicle. I had fifteen hundred dollars that I would put down for a vehicle and that was all I was bringing to the table. I signed the papers as well as my sponsor, and I drove off with a white 2015 Toyota Corolla which I named *White Diamond*. That was my baby.

I got back to the house and called my few friends down to see her and my BFF was ecstatic! I was making my dreams a reality and crossing off my goals. We took pictures around the car, and of course I posted them to Facebook. I was proud of me. Slowly but surely, me and Mr. Brandon, had begun to talk on the phone more and when we saw each other in the meeting we would acknowledge each other, but sit in different rows. We would never sit together.

One day I had went somewhere and got a plate of food to eat while in the meeting. I called him and asked him if he was hungry and he said yes, and I told him I had some food for him. It didn't dawn on me until later that he was a Muslim and didn't eat pork. I had given him the tray and then had to take it back, explaining it was pork chops on the tray. The meeting ended and we left. I took him home then left to go home myself.

It was the weekend and all I had to do was lay in bed and watch TV. Since we were on a first name basis, and not dealing with work, I was able to call him Lorenzo. He was a little quiet and very observant. Lorenzo noticed every little detail about everything. We would talk on the phone for an hour or more then tell each other goodnight.

Lorenzo invited me to go to the mosque with him. I did so that Sunday and enjoyed the lecture that was given. I enjoyed it so much that I decided to come to the class they held for the sisters on Saturday mornings. Each week, I found myself drawn to those meetings.

Lorenzo came to my house one day and we got into an argument. Lorenzo decided that he was going to walk out my door and the building without me escorting him out. The rules of the program were to sign your guest in and out the building. They were not to be wandering around the building by themselves.

He rushed out the door, and I was behind him yelling that he couldn't just do what he wanted to do. He left the building and I signed him out then went back upstairs. I was so damn mad that I took my medication and went to bed. Dozing off, my phone rang and it was him. I didn't answer. I was woozy off the medication, but he kept calling my phone.

When I decided to answer, Lorenzo said he had left his keys in my car and I was jeopardizing his recovery because he didn't have his keys and I wouldn't answer my phone. I told him I would bring the keys to him even though I was intoxicated off my medicine. I was taking two hundred milligrams of Seroquil, and they worked fast. I was tired as shit, but I drove all the way uptown to give this man his keys.

I called and told him where I was, and he kept saying I was in the wrong place. I asked him to direct me, but he was being real difficult. I finally reached him. He got in the car, I gave him the keys, dropped him off, and then I left. I said to myself that I would never get involved romantically with this psycho.

Everything had to be his way. Everyone else had a problem and he didn't. He was well. He didn't need meetings like I did. I said I would never force a meeting on anyone who doesn't want to go. I am only responsible for my own recovery. I didn't attend the Friday meeting for two weeks, not wanting to run into him unless it was by my car.

I knew right then and there that a relationship was not what I needed at that time. He was a bit much for me. He wasn't the kind of person who would come straight out and apologize. He would beat around the bush and do or say some real slick shit out his mouth that was supposed to suffice as an apology.

I was just as stubborn as he was. I knew I had hell on my hands. I was dealing with a Gemini. I'm a Sagittarius, and we really didn't click. At least not as a couple anyway, but God saw otherwise. They always say that if you want to make God laugh tell Him your plans.

One day while working, he came into the office and handed me a bag. The bag contained a Michael Kors brown leather purse. I was not a materialistic or named brand person. I had grown out of that a long time ago. Lorenzo would dress his ass off. Everything he wore from his hat to his shoes matched. I would match my clothes, but I wasn't a fashionista. I mainly wore scrubs Monday through Friday, and on the weekends I would wear T-shirts and boxers. That's because I really didn't get out the house and do anything.

We were now a couple, and we had fallen out quite a few times. He was a Dr. Jekyll-Mr. Hyde type of person. When he was at the mosque, he was so warm, friendly, and such a gentleman. When he was home he was a straight nigga. Going to the mosque regularly helped me understand the person I was dealing with a little better. We all had our demons and we all had our way of dealing with things.

I found out that in the Nation of Islam, we weren't to have or be boyfriend and girlfriend. We were supposed to court one another to really see if that person was for you. Lorenzo and I didn't go through the courting phase. We jumped right in and moved in together. The people in the mosque knew and in order to make this right, we had to recite before an officer the actual facts of Islam, and then we would get married and graduate.

Lorenzo recited before me, but I just couldn't seem to get the hang of it. There was so much to learn and when it was time to recite, we had to know everything from the questions to the answers. I had studied so much that I was exhausted. I spent that weekend at his place. We went out to an all-white affair, and had a ball. When we got back to his place all I wanted to do was go to bed. I wasn't use to staying up late, so my body was tired.

Sunday morning, he went to the mosque and I went home to prepare for my work week.

My birthday was drawing near, and Lorenzo had come to the office bearing gifts for me. My coworkers were in awe at the outfit he bought me. Inside the bag was a burgundy blouse and a pair of black stretch jeans. It was a cute outfit. I thanked him and my office manager asked me where was hers. I snapped my neck so hard that it could've popped off my shoulders. She looked at me and I shrugged it off. Call it jealousy if you want, but I call it being disrespectful, and that's what she was being. I walked outside for a few minutes, gave him a kiss then it was back to work.

My birthday came and went and I was still left to study so that I could recite by the end of December. On December 26th, 2017, I recited and passed and received my X. I was now known as Sherita 2X Washington. On the 28th of December, Lorenzo and I moved into our apartment. Things were beginning to look better for us. We went to the court building at the end of January and filled out the necessary paperwork to obtain our marriage license, and on February 7th, 2018, we were married at the courthouse in DC. We had a few friends and relatives there, and it was the happiest day of my life. I was now, Mrs. Sherita Brandon.

CHAPTER EIGHT

Just like that, my life was changing for the good of Allah. We decided that we would also get married in the mosque, so on February 11th our minister and brother of the Nation of Islam dedicated us as a married couple. We also went to Chicago that month for Saviour's Day and graduated. We were now legal in all aspects. We had a wonderful time there. We met Muslims from all over and heard our minister, The Honorable Louis Farrakhan, speak and we also heard Stephanie Mills sing. I was amazed at how the events of my life were unfolding.

We had rode the bus to Chicago and by the time we hit DC, I had to rush off to work. I had called and told them we were running behind schedule, and they said it would be okay. Adjusting to life as a married woman had its ups and downs. I learned that marriage was just like parenting. It doesn't come with instructions. You have to learn as you go. I can't tell you that everything was peaches and cream because it wasn't. We would argue and curse each other out like dogs. I have pulled a knife on him several times and have even called the police on him to remove him from the household.

I came to realize that Lorenzo has trust issues. He would accuse me of shit and would actually believe I was messing around. I would only go to work, come home, and go to the Friday meeting. He would swear by God Almighty that I was seeing someone there. He accused me of cheating with this guy who was my Facebook friend, who ran in the same circles I have but we just never ran into one another. I told the guy about the S.O.M.E. program, and I told him about the meetings they have on Friday.

This particular Friday, Lorenzo didn't come to the meeting but the other guy did. Now keep in mind, I didn't know him from a can of paint but he recognized me and spoke. I spoke back to him and gave him a hug because that's what we do in meetings. I welcomed him to the group and I went and sat up front since I was a trusted servant and I was also secretary at that particular time.

I had given the guy my phone number and told him if he needed someone to talk to that I was available. I told him that he could also talk with my husband. One day my husband was picking me up from work and my phone rang. Since I had been getting so many scam like calls, I would dismiss it. I answered the phone and the guy said that he pocket dialed me. My husband was like that was strange because no ones phone couldn't straight pocket dial a whole phone number including area code. Lorenzo called the phone number back and they talked, and he found out that   it was the guy from the meeting.

Apparently, he had my name by the phone number, and I never had his. I just gave him mine from being a good person in recovery. My husband blew that all out of proportion, saying I cheated on him and blah blah this, and blah blah that. That was really pissing me off and I pulled a knife on him again. He said he was leaving and taking the marriage certificate to the courthouse and getting a divorce. At that point, I really didn't give two flips about it. Be gone! Get your shit and get out!

I took his set of keys and told him to get out. I told him that I didn't need him because if he didn't throw that guy's name in my face, he would throw my ex-girlfriend's name in my face. I was so freaking sick and tired of hearing that crap. I felt that in his past relationships someone must have done him wrong by cheating on him. I have never cheated in my life. It was the opposite. Everyone cheated on me and I was supposed to be okay with it.

Lorenzo would never share his past relationships with me. I only knew of the female he was with before me. They were engaged to be married and she passed away, but before she left this world she told him to find someone he could share the rest of his life with. Because we're in the Nation of Islam, we're taught to allow the mosque to handle our affairs. Meaning, if a man puts his hands on a woman the F.O.I.'s (Fruit Of Islam) should handle the brother. Any issues we have as a couple should be bought before the minister.

We had a big blow out and again I drew a knife on him and he pushed me. I kept jumping in his face, waiting for him to hit me, so that I could punch holes in the Nation's regulations. We went before the minister and I was hesitant about seeing him. I didn't want to hear anything he had to say. I had to have a sister present and I called my faithful one. That sister had been down for me since I came into the mosque. I could never understand why she was so bent over in helping me get the essential things I needed to be a MGT (Muslim Girl Training).

The conversation began with me. The minister was leaned back in his chair listening to some oldies but goodies, and I felt like he wasn't even listening to what I was saying, but as soon as Lorenzo began to talking he was all ears. This brotherhood seemed powerful and there wasn't anything I could do to separate them from that. Everyone saw things in their own perspective and I could see where this conversation with me giving a person who is seeking recovery my number was going.

The minister felt that the guy was plotting to get next to me and my husband agreed. I just shook my head in disbelief. I was taught in recovery that no suffering addict need ever die! I was always looking for the good in everyone. I was content with being with Lorenzo, but he kept showing doubt and seeing fault in me no matter what I did to ensure him that I was not doing anything.

Lorenzo was an outgoing guy. He liked to dance and the get to gathers that are thrown all year long. I never had a problem with him going out. He would use my car and go to these affairs then pick me up from work since I got off at midnight. What really began bothering me was whenever I got up and wanted to go somewhere, whether it's to the park or a friend's house, he would always say that I'm going to meet my boyfriend. That shit burned me up.

One day he tried to compare me with his childhood friend and I got real upset, maybe even jealous, because here was a woman who actually knew my husband and basically everything about him and I knew little to nothing. I accused him of being with her and that went all the way to the left. I called her and asked her were they involved and it was all because of him comparing me to her. I tried to make amends with her, but she was still a little bitter and I can understand that. After all, they were from the sandbox and I ruined that with just one phone call.

I tried even harder to make amends with her but she was not budging, and again I was fine with that. It was good to know that he saw her at an affair and they hand danced as usual. They were always partners and when I did see them dance, they were having a ball. I never wanted that to end. It's always good to have your friends, so that whenever your relationship screws up they'll be there for you and have your back.

I just knew that I would never be able to change Lorenzo's thoughts or the process of his thoughts, but I felt like when he goes up in his head he gets stuck there. He would imagine the worse about me, and I would do nothing but go to work and come home. I didn't even have a life for real because I was always working. My circle of friends was very small. They would call and ask if I wanted to go out, but usually I couldn't because of my work schedule.

I was able to take time off to go to Ocean City and we had fun, but still argued over whom I was with. It was like if I was not directly under him, I was doing something wrong. I would always be accused. He would see me around one of my gay friends and swear I was cheating. I just couldn't keep doing that with him. He was jealous. He wanted his friends and to hang out and he wanted me at home. I was not a stay at home wife or mother. I liked to venture out. I just didn't. He would always have my car and go places and again I would be stuck at work.

Now this is the hit: He went down to the park where he grew up but got mad when I want to the park to play cards where I use to hang out. There was no difference. They drank and smoked at the park he went to and they definitely drank and smoked at the park I hung out at. To keep the peace, I just didn't go anywhere. I got a phone call saying that I had to come to orientation for a job I applied for. I put in a leave slip for that and also a doctor's appointment. When I asked my office manager about it, she said I was approved to go to my appointment, but the doctor didn't sign off on me going to an orientation. I couldn't understand why he didn't when I had spoken to him about that earlier in the month. I told her I was going anyway and she said that I would deal with the repercussions. I said I guess I will.

The Tuesday came for me to attend the orientation and I went. I was hired to be an on call monitor for S.O.M.E. That evening I received a call from my office manager saying that since I didn't come to work that day, don't come in the next day and that was fine by me. That meant she would have to get her lazy ass up and come in. I already knew she couldn't be on time. For that matter, none of them could touch me as far as coming to work on time and early at that. I was already a step ahead of her. I had already typed up a two weeks' notice so that I could hand it directly to her. As soon as I left from uptown, I went home and rested. It had been a long but eventful day.

The next day, since I didn't have to go in, I made my way to the office to see my manager. I asked where she was and the front office receptionist went and got her. When she came to the front, I had the paper in my hand and extended it out to her. She kept asking what it was, and I just said for her to read it. The office manager finally took the paper from my hand, and when she read it, she could've been bought for a wooden nickel. The look on her face was priceless. I wish I could've caught that moment on camera. That would've been all over Facebook.

She left the front office and went to the back to confer with the doctor's daughter. She asked if the GM knew about the notice. The GM was her brother. I yelled back there and said that I had already emailed him. I told them that was taken care of then I turned and exited the office. That felt so good. It felt so right. Then reality set in. *What was I going to do about having a forty hour a week job?* I would only be an on call person and that meant working on days someone else couldn't. I said a prayer and thought that Allah had bought me this far, and He would take me further.

I still had two weeks to work down there, and I already had my stuff planned. That was bought to an abrupt halt when I received an email from the GM. He said I would get my two week's pay, but I didn't have to worry about coming back. I was alright with that. I was just mad that things didn't happen the way that I planned them. I still continued to look for jobs online then a friend of mine told me about Covenant House. I called and an interview was set for me. When I tell you it was nothing but Allah (God) who opened that door for me, all praises to Him.

Almost two months after I left the doctor's office, I was hired and it paid a little more than the job I had just left so I was blessed in more ways than one. I began training immediately, and I was so glad it was only ten minutes away from my home. The program itself was great. It was helping the youth all over the District of Columbia, Maryland, and Virginia. It was transitional housing for youth, both men and women, ages eighteen to twenty-four. It taught them life skills, money management, hygiene, cooking, and cleaning. The residents lived in an apartment shared with a roommate and they learn how to set boundaries and live in an atmosphere of being on their own in society. The program also had an escrow plan where the residents who are working saved at least thirty percent of their money and allowed it to grow, so that when they're ready to discharge from the program they'll have a nice little nest egg.

I could drive to work, but again I allowed my husband to take me to work and pick me up so that he wouldn't have to be stuck in the house. No matter how hard I tried to keep him happy it was useless. He still made snide remarks about me messing around, and then threw that guy from the meeting up in my face. That had been an ongoing thing with him, and I always fed right into his madness.

I was always taught that if a person keeps accusing you of something, then they're the one doing it. When I said that to him, he always seemed to flip that shit right back on me. I didn't care what he said, someone had to have hurt him pretty bad to where he couldn't trust anyone. He always felt like someone was out to get him or do him wrong. I actually told him that he should seek professional help, but he always said I was the one who needed help. That may have been true, but I saw my psychiatrist regularly and take my medicine prescribed to me for my outbursts.

I told my husband all the time that I don't have to play crazy because I really am. I could spazz out on him, and I wouldn't do a day in jail. They would take me to CPEP (Comprehensive Psychiatric Emergency Program), give me a shot, and I would be back to work at my scheduled time. There were days that I wouldn't take my meds, and I would feel okay. Sometimes I would feel a little spaced out, but I was content until he fucked with me and then I hit a thousand in one point one seconds. I really feel he knew it bothered me, and doing that to me was just the highlight of his day. I think he loved when I got overdramatic and lashed out then pulled knives on him.

I can remember when I had just fixed him some breakfast and he got to talking shit. I went in the kitchen faster than Flash Gordon, pulled out a knife and swung it at him. He dropped his whole plate of food. I wanted to laugh in his face so hard, but I turned and walked out the room. I slammed doors and threw glass, especially picture frames and vases. That was my thing.

I didn't throw them directly at him, but nonetheless, I tried to get my point across. I would then go to the linen closet and get a blanket then sleep in the front room.

There was one time that I actually was about to sleep in my car. It was tempting, but I just didn't trust my area of residency. Therefore, I smoked my cigarette in my car, turned the music up on blast, and chilled. Once I smoked another cigarette, I went upstairs and went to sleep. I just wanted him to be gone away from me. He would always throw up in my face that he was going to the courthouse and taking the license then leaving. Boy bye! I always told him that I know how to take care of myself. I don't need anyone to validate me. I was doing good before I met him and I would be alright if not better once he left.

*****

April rolled around and usually I got in a funky mood because it was my mom's birthday month (April 30th), and I would act out. I braced myself for the moment to come. I called my CSW and talked to my psychiatrist. I decided I was going to get a puppy. My longtime friend/sister, who I met in North Carolina, was breeding dogs. She had some puppies and when she sent me the pictures, I knew exactly which one was going to be mine. She and her husband drove to DC from Charlotte while heading to Texas.

I was so excited when I met them outside. There were three puppies in the backseat, and they were ready to roam about. The other two puppies went to my husband's childhood friends. They were so lovable and I knew I was going to spoil this pup rotten. We sat around and talked then I fixed them a plate of food. I knew they had to be hungry after driving nonstop, except to let the pups drink water and use the bathroom.

Right from the beginning, Rockie was a handful. He wanted to be everywhere all at once. His brothers were just as bad. They were getting into everything they could, but it was fun watching them. One of my husband's friends came and got his fur baby and we had to deliver the other one. His friend called and told him that she didn't want the dog. He pooped and stuff was moving around in his stool. We told her it was worms. They would definitely have to go to the vet as soon as possible.

I took Rockie to get his shots and he was excited to be in there. The staff was loving on him and he ate that right on up. When we got back home, I allowed him to run around for a bit. I put puppy pads down so he could get use to going on them. Trying to take him outside was my biggest challenge. He didn't know how to climb up and down the steps, so I had to pick him up and carry him. I learned that the dog was playful and had mood swings just like me. He was a Sagittarian also and born on December 14th.

We were going to get along just fine. I took him out so much that he was trained within a month's time. He slept in the carryon bag he came down in, and I had him sleeping in the bedroom by the entrance. He would cry a lot, just like a newborn baby and I would take him out and rock him until he was ready to go to sleep. I finally got him a cage then my husband put him out in the front room. Rockie didn't like that one bit. He would cry and cry until I came to his rescue. I would even sleep on the couch so he knew that I was close by.

Months rolled on by and before I knew it, my husband's birthday was here. We went out to eat and had a great time together. We actually had become civil towards one another. I gave him roses, a couple of cards with money inside, and good sex. Months had gone by, and I was enjoying my new job. We were in the process of moving the residents to a new facility and a lot of people hate change. I was one of them. Instead of being ten minutes away from work, I was now twenty to twenty-five minutes away. I was still on the four PM to twelve AM shift and yes, my husband still took me to and from work until we got mad at one another then I would drive myself.

I enjoyed the ride to work for the most part. I would blast my music and smoke a cigarette then just let the air blow away that negativity. Before I got out the car, I would say a prayer and ask Allah to get rid of the nonsense and fill my head with good thoughts. I couldn't go to work with a negative attitude. Those youths needed our undivided attention, and I had to be strong for them even when I wasn't for myself.

The time was moving fast and before I knew it, I was celebrating my four year anniversary. That was going to be a great one because my Aunt Jane finally got to come to hear how the program works and hear stories from other addicts and what worked for them and how they overcame addiction. She was fascinated by it all. She hugged me and told me how proud of me she was and I smiled. Knowing all the shit I did during my addiction made me wonder why was my family still here for me after I stole a lot of their money, clothes, jewelry, etc. They should have dismissed me a long time ago, but they held on to hope.

It was a great day for me. I took my aunt's hand and told her how much I loved her and appreciated her and said I would be there for her if she ever needed me. She hugged me and kissed me gently on my cheek then smiled. During that phase of my life, I was still doing step work. I was just finishing step three when my sponsor asked me to read step four for thirty days. That step had me cringing on the inside. I was about to discover who Sherita really was, like it or not.

Before I read any step, I pray, asking God to be the leader and allow me to follow through on what I need to do to help myself in my recovery. I asked my sponsor what was that step all about and she told it was about purging and cleaning. *Okay, I can go with that,* I thought to myself. She also asked me to take a piece of paper and divide it in half then write down my assets and liabilities. I already knew my liabilities would outweigh my assets.

As I began to write, I saw that my assets were outweighing my liabilities, and still some of my assets were my liabilities and vice versa. I really wasn't this bad person people made me out to be, in fact I was the total opposite. I found laughter and fun in a lot of things. I even laughed at my own quirkiness. I loved people and I loved hard. I was very open and crystal clear on who I am and not who you want me to be. Now there had been numerous occasions where I felt like an outsider. I could never be with the *in* crowd because I felt I didn't meet their criteria, and that's why I mostly stayed at home away from the functions. My grand sponsor told me the week before that if I'm a part of narcotics anonymous, I am a part of the so called *in* crowd.

Each of us had come in the rooms by way of drugs, alcohol, or any mind altering chemical. We each had our story and sometimes that person's story happened to be yours. Now as time moved on more things had happened and I had to remember that was *life on life's terms.* Things appeared to be better with me. I took my meds regularly and if I missed a dose, I called my CSW and told him in case something happened to me during the course of the day.

*****

February rolled around and we (my husband and I) had made it to through our first year of marriage. During the past eleven months, I was quite sure we would have killed one another, but we're still here only through the grace and mercy of Allah. All praises be to Him. It was almost Saviour's Day and me and few sisters were discussing our travel arrangements. We were trying to decide whether we were going to catch a plane, ride a bus that was chartered, or drive. I wasn't planning on going this year because Ocean City was around the corner, and we (my husband and I) needed to save for that trip.

I can remember in my MGT class, we were sewing a tam and preparing to make an outfit when I asked one of the instructors for some help and she totally ignored me. I went to her again, and she had rolled her eyes as if I were asking her too many times, so I packed up my belongings and left the mosque without saying anything to anyone. I was determined that I wasn't coming back until I was good and ready because had I stayed it would've been ugly.

I went home and told my husband about it and he said I needed to learn how to use the chain of command. I wasn't ready to hear any of that from him. I felt he was taking their side, so I got in my feelings and stayed away. My husband was ready to celebrate six years of recovery and I was to be the MC. The anniversary was real nice. In fact, over seventy people were in attendance. He and I were dressed in burgundy. I wore my Muslim attire and he wore a burgundy suit, looking like new money. He had a great time and you could actually see the glow in his eyes and upon his face. After the anniversary, we served cake and punch and mingled for a moment with friends then went home.

April arrived and we were excited about going to Ocean City. I didn't know where Lorenzo got his shit from but he picked an argument. Then I said that I'm not going. I told him if I did go it would only be to pick up my two registrations, sell them, and then leave. Lorenzo said that he would find a way up there. *More power to you,* I thought to myself. Once again Satan's spawn attacked me and I was fed up for real. I was pissed because I had spent my money on buying him a registration pack and a ticket to the Go-Go, and he was still ungrateful as hell.

My sponsee's sister and another friend who was in the program with me asked if they could ride, and I said they could. I explained they could put their luggage in the trunk, but if they had a carryon bag to keep that with them. Lorenzo decided that he was going and that he could drive. I said okay and left it alone. I knew I was going to have to put on a façade around my friends, but I would get pass that crap.

The day of the trip, I was calling to make sure everyone was in place so that there wouldn't be a problem or delay when it was time to roll out. Since I was working and my shift didn't end until midnight, Lorenzo would have to pick them up and then come get me. I called my sponcee sister and asked her would she be ready and she said she would. I called my other friend and asked her the same thing and received the same answer.

Now, it was almost time for me to get off, and my husband was calling me and I was trying to reach the ladies and no one seemed to want to answer their phone. Finally, my friend said that she was ready. My sponcee sister finally called me back and said that she was already on her way to Ocean City. *What? Seriously? This chick didn't even have the decency to call me and tell me that she had another way there,* I thought to myself. I had it in my mind that when I saw her, I was going to curse her the hell out. She was an inconsiderate ass chick!

While on the road and heading to Ocean City, we made only one stop and that was to use the bathroom and get gas. We made good timing. There was no traffic whatsoever, just a few cars here and there. We made it to our hotel and checked in. Due to my friend's room not being ready until eleven AM, we let her crash on the other bed in our room. We all fell asleep and when we got up, we hurried over to the convention center to get a spot in line for registration. It actually didn't take long to get through the line. I was in and out before I knew it.

After we received our package, we went back to our room then took my friend to her hotel. I was ready to get a few more hours of sleep. I woke up still feeling sluggish, so I made a cup of coffee and headed out. When we got back to the center, I signed up for different things to do like, being on the hug squad, serenity keeper, and going to meetings. I always looked forward to the woman's rap. I saw a lot of my friends and we snapped pictures and had light conversations, promising to meet back up later. I sold my ticket to the Go-Go. I really wasn't feeling it this year. I stayed at the hotel and took my medicine, played games on my phone then I went to sleep.

Once I finished hugging everybody from all over the world, I went and sat down in the lobby area. My husband was nowhere to be found and no matter how many times I rang his phone, he couldn't seem to hear it but he got mad when you didn't answer yours. Go figure that shit out because I sure as hell couldn't. Saturday had arrived and it was almost time for the big countdown of clean time. I always look forward to the countdown. There was so much clean time in that big room. Once that was over it was time for the Go-Go.

We left the center so that he could take me back to the hotel so he could attend the dance. I took my medicine so I could be good and ready to go to sleep. I let him keep the car so he could get back to the hotel without asking anyone else for a ride. He was off and I was in the bed with my games at the ready. I didn't know what time he came in and really didn't care. I was done with that trip and vowed that I would not be going next year.

Now, it was Sunday morning and we're packing our belongings up so we could go eat breakfast at the hotel's diner, which was free. Once we finished, we called my friend to let her know we were on our way to get her. After picking her up, we went to the convention center for the last time to get the last meeting in and say goodbye to all our friends. We wished everyone safe traveling graces and mercy on their routes back home.

We only made one stop on the way back and that was to get a cup of coffee and smoke a cigarette. We made it back to DC in record time. We dropped my friend off then headed on home. I was so glad to be back to my place of residency. Lorenzo went to pick up Rockie from his brother's place and when they returned home, I was so happy to see my baby. He jumped all over me and I grabbed, hugged, and rocked him in my arms. I loved that dog!

That day went by fast and before long, I was in the bed and asleep. I was off the next day, but still managed to go to a meeting. When I came home, me and Rockie took a walk and came in and played around for a few minutes, then I showered and laid on the bed to watch some NetFlix. I found myself ready to doze off, so I had to get up and put my puppy in his cage so I can go to sleep and he can as well. My husband came in and I tried to stay woke, but due to my medication, I was out for the count.

The next morning, waking up and feeling refreshed and revived, I took my pup out for his morning ritual then came in and cooked me and Lorenzo some breakfast. We laid around all day and it felt good. Later that evening, I showered, to prepare myself for work the next day, and cooked dinner. Once we finished, I walked the dog and me and the hubby cuddled up and watched television. As I went about my work week, Lorenzo continued to take me to and from work and still hung out with his friends. Once I get off work, I just want to sleep.

Here it was May, and I'd been employed with Covenant House for a year. I still get hours as an on call monitor at S.O.M.E., whenever it's available. I enjoy my line of work, it's just that my supervisor always seems to find fault in my decisions I make as a residential advisor. He's much younger than I am and the youths gravitate to him more than the rest of us staff. When we as staff members try to implement the rules of the program to the youths, we're being shut down by him. They now get rewarded for doing wrong. Many get so many curfew violations, then turn around and ask him for an extension, overnight or weekend pass and he grants their wish. I ask him about it and it seems to be a problem when asking him such questions. I just leave it alone. I'm damned if I do and damned if I don't.

Damn!

Hello June, this month has been great. My husband finally got his own ride and also celebrated his birthday. I told him his gift from me was to pay his insurance, registration and take him out to eat. I still managed to do more, but hey, that's my husband and that's what we do for each other. I was glad I looked online and found a seller in Maryland. We called and talked to the man and a couple of days later, he was driving it home. All praises be to Allah! One Sunday, I decided I would go to the mosque with my husband. I got all dressed up in my white garment and was escorted to car by my husband, and we headed to the mosque. Once there, I parked in the parking lot of the 7-11, and we walked across Branch and Pennsylvania Avenue, to the mosque.

Once I entered, I should've known something was amiss. I was called into the entrance to be checked and afterwards, a sister asked me to step to the side for a minute, she needed to speak to me. I waited until she returned and when she did, she said that I haven't been to the mosque since December, and I told her that was a lie. I had been in February, when a few of us sisters was discussing Saviour's Day. She said according to the records, it indicates I have been away more than six months and I would have to meet with her and the captain when he's available. I tried to contain my composure, but slowly and surely, my alter ego was coming out. The sister asked for my number and I snapped and told her get it from another sister then I was being escorted out. I said I'm not leaving until I see my husband and tell him this shit. A sister went and got my husband for me and as I was telling him, he was saying, "Go ahead out the door Sherita!" I looked at him in disbelief and went on out. We're supposed to cross at the light, but I was livid and chose to cross right in the middle of the street with oncoming traffic. I heard my husband call me, but I ignored him, figuring he was with this crap. I walked faster to my car and got in. I was pulling off, when he yelled out my name. The look I had given him was a look of disgust. At that time and moment, I hated the mosque, the people, and what they stood for. I didn't care about returning. I don't need a mosque to talk to God. He is everywhere and I stood on that belief. I was mad because my husband didn't have my back and I felt alone. He got in the car and said he was going to get his truck so he could go back. That's where my sick thinking began. If it had been the opposite, I would've left out with my husband and we both would've left together. I was actually glad to be home. I could go back to sleep and ready myself for work at four PM. By the time Lorenzo came in, I was getting myself ready to go, and yes I was still mad as hell, not only at the mosque, but at him also. He came in talking this stuff I really didn't want to hear and at that present time, I didn't give two flips about the mosque or returning. I talked to a sister I call my savior. She is always there for me no matter what. I told her all that happened and she said she's going to get this meeting taken care of as soon as possible. I said okay and left for work. A week had passed and the call finally came through for me to meet with the first officer and the captain. It was on a Sunday, so I didn't wear my white garment. I wasn't exactly back in, so why dress the part? I dressed in a turquoise garment and left my head uncovered. They asked me to have a seat in the mosque's sanctuary and they'll be ready for me soon. It was now time for collection of donations. My husband asked me to go in half with him on a one hundred dollar donation. I rolled my eyes. I wasn't ready to give them my money after escorting me out. I've been put out of many places, and now I can add the mosque to my long list. I had to laugh to keep from crying. I gave the donation, and as I went to the lobby to make the transaction, they informed me that they were ready for me downstairs. It was hotter than Jamaican Jerk wings down there! I was hoping this wouldn't take long. As I approached the room where we would be, it was empty. The captain still hadn't made it downstairs. I sat out in the opening and the sister gave me a scarf to drape my head. She informed me that I was still going in front of a brother and needed to be covered. I was like whatever. The captain finally made his way to us. We were seated, and I felt like I was sitting before the Judge, hoping and wishing for a lighter sentence. After he read off the charges, I disagreed with being gone for six months, however, they went by what the book said. I felt someone was trying to sabotage me and assassinate my character. Trust me, there's a lot of jealousy in the mosque. Not just from the women, but the men as well and I believe they have more jealousy amongst each other than the women. I wasn't trying to be in no "social circle," I just wanted to learn my teachings of the Honorable Elijah Muhammad and The Honorable Minister Louis Farrakhan. I wanted to know more about the teachings of The Nation Of Islam and the difference between them, the Orthodox, and the Sunni's. I practiced Islam for over fourteen years, and I was a Sunni Muslim. I received my teachings in the prison system and I enjoyed what I learned and read. Now, I'm in a whole new different light, with a different perspective on Muslims. I'm not going to sit here and tell you I pray five times a day and I fast and I do all the things an upright Muslim is supposed to do, because I don't. I went back to smoking cigarettes and that's a big no in the Nation. I strive every day to do what's pleasing in the eyes of Allah. Now, I agreed to attend mosque on Sundays when permissible and give my donation and attend a group during the week. I chose to do the group on Friday since that's an off day for me and I can alternate with my Friday night recovery meeting. Now, here I am, sitting at my work place pondering over some shit that just went down earlier today. Today is July 24th, 2019, and I got up early to go get my hair braided. I was due to meet with a staff member at S.O.M.E., but was told to wait until later. I went over there after one PM, and there was an emergency going on, and I was asked to come back next Tuesday. I said okay and left. Since I was close by my job, I stopped at my favorite Chinese place, to get something to eat and a large cup of ice. While waiting for my food, I received a text from my SRA (Senior Residential Advisor), or to put it simpler, my supervisor. This is how the conversation went:

He: Ms. Braannddoonnnnnn

He: Mrs.

He: Although your hours will be only Saturday and Sunday 4p-12a, I found twelve hour shift on Wednesday 8p-8a wanted to offer you to help make up some hours. Let me know A.S.A.P. if you can work this shift starting August 1st before they offer it to someone else.

I had to read this about four times before I texted back.

Me: Who's doing 8am-4pm Saturday and Sunday mornings?

Me: Where's the 12 hour shift on Wednesday?

He: That's the double I was try'n (his spelling of trying) to get you to do, but couldn't.

He: Yes it's Wednesday.

Me: There's no way I can get another day added? This is taking away from my livelihood.

He: I'll speak with them again and try. Was that a no for Wednesday.

Me: Is it at ROP?

He: Sanctuary. I believe Yuma Street.

Me: How will my timesheet reflect that since they couldn't switch my time to work Safe Haven?

He: Think you couldn't work SH due to certain grants and or trainings or something like that, nothing to do with pay.

Me: I think this is wrong. I was there before Mr. and should've been offered a full time. How did this come to play? Was it your recommendation?

He: They asked me everyone's schedule, I sent it in.. told me to inform everyone what I did. They didn't ask nor did I give a recommendation. This starts August 1st.

He: Are you confirming you can work the 12 hour Wednesday shift?

Me: No thank you.

He: Ok.

This is some bullshit! I've been at this job for a little over a year, and I am full time, working four days a week at thirty-two hours. He claims that since I didn't have the fifth day, I was only able to do only weekend shift from four PM to twelve AM. What I don't understand is where does the seniority come in? I've been here longer than the other person, and yet they give him the fifth day. After texting back and forth, I was pissed and exhausted and ready to go. I sat in the office at work and contemplated on whether I should stay or go. For all that, he can come do this freaking shift. It's his building and he should take up the slack since he does nothing anyway but allow these youth to do whatever they want. That's why they're so out of control. You can't say too much to them about anything because they'll call or text him and next thing you know, you're sitting in the back office in a meeting. What gets to me the most is when they buck up at the staff and we ask for a meeting, it takes forever, if we even get one. So… Life still goes on. I will continue to go about my days seeking employment and hope to find something even better. The good that came from this is that S.O.M.E., has offered me to work three days a week which gives me twenty-four hours. Since I'm on call, I can't have more than twenty-nine hours a week, but I will get as close as possible if not the whole twenty-nine. I'll stay with Covenant House momentarily and then it's off to new beginnings. When things like this use to happen to me, I would go get drunk and high and say the black national anthem, "F it!" Not today. Today, I've learned that I can talk about these issues and get past them. I do know that Allah didn't bring me this far to leave me. He has something else in store for me. Be it Community Connections, Safe Haven, or back in the Medical Field, I'll just continue to hold on and keep the faith. The Bible says just have enough faith as a mustard seed and I do. Life will throw some curve balls, fast balls, and some strike outs, but it's up to you on how you handle things. I hope my story has helped someone deal with the demons that are trapped inside of their bodies and know that life holds a lot of guarantees. One guarantee for me is that, "I don't have to use, no matter what comes my way!" Insha Allah, (If it's the will of God), I will receive my Associate's degree for Addiction/Psychology in August and in October, I will be celebrating my five year anniversary and I will be in another job by then. You have to speak things into existence and believe. I do. Before I close, I just want to say, if you're an addict and you're reading this book, give yourself a chance. You'll find out that's the best decision you could ever make for yourself. Whether you're in recovery or not, share that pain. It only helps you to heal and grow… I did!

Picking Up the Pieces

Picking up the pieces and starting your life over seems so far fetched that it seems impossible to do, but you actually can. Living by the cliché one day at a time really makes sense. We're so quick to try to fix things instead of letting things be the way that they are intended to be at that moment.

Nothing in this world is by coincidence. It all starts with Allah (God) and it end with him. Until we get it in our minds that we can only accept people the way that they are and were they are, we will never get far in life.

Through this process of mine, I've learned to lower my expectations and increase my acceptance. That means that I can't expect a person to be on my level when they are not and vice versa. We have to deal with the situation the way it presents itself. I used to place people on a pedestal and they were not meant to be there. I expected so much from them, and yet again I was left disappointed.

Now, I accept people how they are and at where they are in their life. I don't think I'm better than anyone. I just think that I'm better off. I drive pass the park and say to myself keep it moving, knowing that there's nothing left out there for me. I still see most of the people that were on their journey when I was on mine from 2011 to 2014.

They're still sitting in the park at the same time on the old benches and doing the same thing. I just made a conscience decision to do something different and I get better results.

The life I'm living is fairly well and I can't complain. Every day isn't a good day, but I survive it without the use of drinking or drugs. Today, I have learned that I can talk about what I have been through and not dwell on it. The longer I stay stuck in a situation means the more that I am to give it time to conjure.

A HUSTLA'Z LIFE
PART TWO: REVENGE

Having successfully served out his one hundred and twenty day probation, Hannibal is free move about the country and expand his criminal empire. He has devised a plan that will bring a level of anonymity to himself and the top-level people he has around him. He has also found a way to eliminate the competition and consolidate their operations into his.

However, just like in the game of baseball, life throws him a curve ball. Hannibal takes out a couple of individuals that were trying to move in on some his territory. He thinks that the guys he killed were just some small-time hustla'z with oversized dreams. Little did he know those small-time hustla'z he murdered had powerful friends. A chain reaction of events propelled by the thirst for revenge begins to take place that could cost him more than territory, it could cost him his life.

A HUSTLA'Z LIFE PART THREE:

MIAMI

Made in the USA
Lexington, KY
05 December 2019